THE
JOSHUA
PROJECT

Three overlooked biblical strategies
for parents and grandparents to
strengthen their family's faith

JANIS HUTCHINSON

THE
JOSHUA
PROJECT

*Three overlooked biblical strategies
for parents and grandparents to
strengthen their family's faith*

JANIS HUTCHINSON

Cross and Pen Ministries
EVERETT, WA

Published by EDK Books and
Distributed by EDK Distribution, LLC

Published by EDK Books and
Distributed by EDK Distribution, LLC
edkbookdistribution.com | edkbooksanddistribution@gmail.com | (206) 227-8179

The Joshua Project
Copyright © 2021 by Janis Hutchinson
Cross and Pen Ministries - Everett, WA

Unless otherwise indicated, all Scripture quotations are taken from the New Living Translation version of the Bible, copyright © 1996, 2004, 2007, 2015, copyright 2015 by Tyndale House Foundation. Tyndale House Publishers Inc., Carol Stream, Illinois 60188.

Italics, brackets, and/or other formatting added to Scripture quotations are the author's emphasis.

Other Scripture versions are taken from the following sources:

English Standard Version (ESV) ESV® Permanent Text Edition® (2016). Copyright © 2001 by Crossway Bibles, a publishing ministry of Good News Publishers.

New International Version ®, (NIV), copyright © 1973, 1978, 1984, 2011 by Biblica, Inc.®.

The King James Version (KJV) Public domain.

The Amplified Bible (AMP) Copyright © 2015 by The Lockman Foundation, La Habra, CA 90631.

The Amplified Bible, Classic Edition (AMPC) Copyright © 1954, 1958, 1962, 1964, 1965, 1987 by The Lockman Foundation.

The Living Bible (TLB), copyright © 1971 by Tyndale House Foundation. Tyndale House Publishers Inc., Carol Stream, Illinois 60188.

New American Standard Bible (NASB), Copyright © 1960, 1962, 1963, 1968, 1971, 1972, 1973, 1975, 1977, 1995 by The Lockman Foundation.

New King James Version® (NKJV), copyright © 1982 by Thomas Nelson.

The Message, by Eugene H. Peterson (MSG). Copyright © 1993, 1994, 1995, 1996, 2000, 2001, 2002, 2018.

10 9 8 7 6 5 4 3 2 1

Printed in the United States of America

ISBN 978-1-9560650-0-8

Design: Julie K. Lee

Every parent and grandparent needs to read this book. Hutchinson provides a modern version of the three strategies God mandated to Joshua that instructs Israel's parents and grandparents on how to pass on their testimonies of him. This shows today's parents and grandparents how to combat today's anti-god secularism that is influencing our children and grandchildren to leave the faith. She presents an effective and compelling method on how to pass on our faith stories about God's reality, with step-by-step instructions and illustrations from using this plan with her own children and grandchildren.

—Josh D. McDowell, author

Startling numbers of youth and young adults are walking away from Christianity after having been raised in Christian homes. For all who, like myself, are deeply concerned about the vanishing American church, Janis Hutchinson's book is a 'must read.' *The Joshua Project* is filled with data that is fresh and relevant, and author Hutchinson provides realistic solutions that are practical and most of all—Biblical. I appreciate how she emphasizes the priceless value of grandparents, when it comes to preserving (and nurturing) a families' Biblical foundations. She backs up everything with Scripture, noting that Israel's connection to the True God was often passed on to the youth by older generations, recounting to the upcoming people all that God had done! This book is so right for our times! Adults, parents, church leaders, and all who care about the soul and future of our nation . . . please read this unique and well-done book. I believe that God will use this to change many lives!

—Alex McFarland, President, Truth For A New Generation

Not only does God define in the Bible what a parent and grandparent is to do, but He also describes how parents and grandparents are to make disciples and pass on faith to future generations. God doesn't call parents and grandparents to a task without telling us how to accomplish the outcomes He desires. The Joshua Project explores a number of God's methods in Scripture and will equip you to share your faith story so that the next generation knows, loves, and serves Christ. Pick up a copy today and bless the children and grandchildren in your life!

—Dr. Josh Mulvihill, author of *Biblical Grandparenting,*
Executive Dir. of Church & Family Ministry at RenewaNation,
and provides leadership to Gospel Shaped Family

Are you at a loss on how to influence and strengthen your children and grand-children in today's anti-God culture? Hutchinson's book provides a practical much-needed solution. With step-by-step instructions and illustrations, she shows parents and grandparents how to practice Joshua's three strategies, pass on personal faith, and instill confidence in God. Based on Hutchinson's success-ful testing with her own children and grandchildren, this is a must read.

—Dr. Warren Haynes, author of *Discipleship Uncomplicated*,
National Director of the ADVANCE Program for Gateway Seminary
of the Southern Baptist Convention

Personal stories are one of the most powerful ways to pass along a legacy of faith. As a new "Mimi," I hope to encourage my grands in their faith. Janis Hutchin-son's inspiring and practical book, *The Joshua Project*, provides the tools and personal examples to help parents and grandparents share their testimonies. Her three-fold-approach shows the reader how to document family faith stories in a way that will generate deeper spiritual conversations and memorialize per-sonal God moments. If you hope to share the great things God has done in your life with your kids or grandkids, you will want to read and apply the strategies presented in The Joshua Project.

—Lori Wildenberg, licensed parent and family educator,
national speaker, podcaster, and author of 5 parenting books
including *The Messy Life of Parenting: Powerful and Practical Ways
to Strengthen Family Connections*

The Joshua Project is a treasure that delighted and motivated me as I read it. Who among us doesn't want to leave a legacy of faith to our children and grandchil-dren? We know of the biblical commands to do just that. And yet few of us know a practical and memorable way to spark conversations with them, much less how to begin to make sure the landmark events of faith in our lives can endure in simple written form. This book gives step by step instructions and inspiring examples from the author's own remarkable experiences and from those of her faithful children and grandchildren.

—Latayne C. Scott, PhD., author of over two dozen published books

I very much like Hutchinson's approach to the important role of grandparenting and passing on to their grandchildren their own life's experiences and their own personal testimonies to what God has done in their lives and the lives of others. This is exactly what God commands us to teach our grandchildren (i.e., Exodus 13 and Joshua 4). With parents as busy as they are today, grandparents may be the only ones who will stand in the gap between God and the world, and children will quickly forget God when we forget to proclaim all He has done in our lives, and still yet to do.

—**Pastor Jack Wellman, author of** *Teaching Children the Gospel*

Valuable and insightful, *The Joshua Project* offers powerful insight to harness personal testimony to challenge, grow, and inspire the next generation. Our faith stories can revitalize and refresh as we teach our children and grandchildren to trust in the Lord with all their hearts. Get ready for practical tools to pass your faith down to the next generation.

—**Lauren Hunter, author of** *Leaving Christian Science:*
10 Stories of New Faith in Jesus Christ

Christian grandparents are mandated by Scripture to actively pass on their faith to their families, but many lack the practical tools to do that effectively. Janis Hutchinson's book, *The Joshua Project*, provides strategies, practical instructions and examples, and personal illustrations that will equip such grandparents to fulfill their biblical role. Based upon the story of Joshua and his efforts to help the children of Israel remember God and His works, *The Joshua Project* is a wonderful, beneficial tool for grandparents that thoroughly fleshes out what telling faith stories looks like.

—**Larry Fowler, Founder, Legacy Coalition**

CONTENTS

SECTION ONE

Create Your Joshua Project

STAGE 1

STAGE 2

STAGE 3

SECTION TWO

Examples of Testimonies for A Joshua Project

Be careful never to forget what you yourself have seen
Do not let these memories escape from your mind as long as you live!
And be sure to pass them on to your children and grandchildren . . .
Do this as long as you live.

—Deut. 4:9; 31:13

I'm thanking you, GOD, from a full heart,
I'm writing the book on your wonders.
I'm whistling, laughing, and jumping for joy;
I'm singing your song, High God.

—Ps. 9:1–2 MSG

INTRODUCTION

Why should you read *The Joshua Project?* How can this book possibly be different from the dozens of books you may have already read on Christian parenting and grandparenting? Because this book is different. Be prepared to learn something new.

The *Joshua Project* will alert parents and grandparents to a powerful biblical tool many Christian families are neglecting—the sharing of personal faith stories. But it's not just the verbalization of them. It includes the incorporation of two other strategies. Here's why this is a necessity.

Families today are facing an epidemic crisis with their youth. Today's post-truth culture, with its mythologizing of God and denigration of absolutes, is destroying faith and sweeping tweens, teens, and young adults into moral and spiritual chaos. Societal ideologies are exerting a stronger influence on our youth than the traditional Christian teachings they are receiving at home or church.

The result is that many are leaving the church after high school graduation, with 63 percent saying they no longer believe Jesus is the Son of God, and 51 percent viewing Jesus' resurrection and God's reality as myths.[1] Though some may return to the faith of their parents, 69 percent will remain gone unless something is done.[2]

A Barna report rightly warns families who are hoping to ensure "a vibrant, lasting faith in the next generation," that the "current state of affairs is not promising."[3]

Parents and grandparents cry, "What more can we do, besides read the Bible with our children and send them to church?"

The need, therefore, is for a fresh, new biblical model for teaching children and grandchildren in the home that will strengthen their faith in a more persuasive and compelling way. This book provides that model.

The *Joshua Project* instructs parents and grandparents on how to employ Joshua's nearly forgotten three-staged strategy of combining writing, creating memorials, and verbalizing that God mandated for Israel. However, the first of these three methods, "writing," is not what you may be picturing.

It is not talking about recording your testimonies in a journal (although this should be done). Rather, it is a special written presentation of selected faith stories placed in the home, visible to all, and designed to correlate with created "memorials," both aimed at piquing curiosity and invoking children and grand-children to ask questions. Chapter 2 explains this procedure in detail.

God's intention for his remarkable plan was to show Israel's parents and grandparents how to repeatedly confirm his existence, glorify his name and to effectively present, promote, pass on, and preserve, their faith testimonies to their children and grandchildren, not only for the then-living generation but also for the yet-unborn.

A modern version of Joshua's plan was created by the author and tested on her family. The effect was more than gratifying. It resulted in her children's and grandchildren's statements (included in the book) of how it deepened their faith and renewed awareness of God's reality. The plan was so effective, it confirmed that her innovative plan would work for other parents and grandparents.

Why Are Grandparents Involved?

According to a Barna study, young people consider their grandparents the greatest potential influences in their lives, ranking just behind their parents.[4]

God specifically included them in his plan. Having lived longer, they often have more personal faith-building testimonies to relate than parents. God knew their testimonies could carry a powerful impact in strengthening grandchildren's faith.

This responsibility is not to be ignored. Grandparents, says Dr. Josh Mulvihill, author of Biblical Grandparenting, should "busy themselves with two activities, telling and teaching" about the glorious deeds of God and the wonders he has performed in their own lives.[5] But here is their dilemma.

The Dilemma of Grandparents

Few grandparents understand their God-mandated role in cultivating the faith of their grandchildren. They believe, as Dr. Mulvihill points out, that they should keep a low profile and not interfere in their children's family.[6] This is not what God intended.

Further, they wonder, "What can we offer that parents or the church can't?" Many also become stumped when the young children they once read Bible stories to outgrow that stage. Nevertheless, regardless of children's ages, whether small children, tweens, teens, or young adults, the objective remains the same. The sharing of personal faith stories by grandparents must continue to verify

God's reality and reassure grandchildren that, as in Bible times, God is still actively working in today's modern world, and is present in their lives.

The Dilemma of Parents

Parents generally do not know how to engender faith in their children, says Scott McConnell, executive director of LifeWay Research. "Churchgoing parents want to pass on their faith to their kids—and to see their children make that faith their own . . . but they don't always know how best to make that happen."[7] They often think their only options are to make sure their children attend church, and read the Bible with them. Too few do both.

The Power of Personal Testimonies

Testimonies from parents and grandparents produce a decisive effect. When faced with spiritual and moral challenges, or confrontations about God, children and grandchildren will remember the memorable testimonies told them that verify God's love, goodness, and immediate availability. They may not be able to recite a specific Scripture, but they will say, when recalling the faith stories, "I know the testimonies of what God did in my parents' and grandparents' lives are true; so, God has to be real and is there for me."

Your personal faith stories will equip present and future generations to have an unshakeable faith in God's reality, substantiate scriptural promises, and empower them to contend against the persuasive pressures challenging them. If parents and grandparents ignore this responsibility, the influences of today's secular culture may shatter a family's best-laid plans to keep their children strong in the faith.

What Does the Joshua Project Specifically Provide?

Parents and grandparents will more fully grasp their responsibility to build the faith of their children and grandchildren through sharing personal testimonies of God. Also, through the presentation of Scripture, they will understand to a greater extent the importance of following the same three-structured plan God instituted from the beginning, writing, creating memorials, and verbalization.

More than just motivational and faith-building, *The Joshua Project* is a how-to book providing step-by-step instructions. Readers will be shown how to apply Joshua's three strategies for each faith story to invoke questions from children and grandchildren no matter how old they are. Pictures of memorials from the author's own Joshua Project are provided as examples in chapters 7 and 8, showing how to match them with the subject of each faith story they represent.

Beginning in chapter 9 to the end are also examples taken from the author's Joshua Project of the types of testimonies to include in a Joshua project. They show not only how to write them, but how to include confirming Scriptures—a necessary ingredient because scripture needs to confirm the trustworthiness of the event.

You will also learn how to use modern resources, including a last will and testament, that will guarantee your many faith stories will survive your demise and be transmitted to future generations.

My hope is that you will follow this biblical pattern and use the contemporary ideas set forth in *The Joshua Project*, not only to comply with God's commandment but also to make a deeper and longer lasting impact on the faith of your children, grandchildren, and future posterity.

—**Janis Hutchinson**

SECTION ONE
CREATE YOUR JOSHUA PROJECT

CHAPTER 1
Joshua's Solution: Our Testimonies Must Not Die!

Thank the LORD! Praise his name! Tell the nations what he has done.
Let them know how mighty he is!
—Isa. 12:4

What if you had a problem God could never solve? That was my dilemma. I couldn't imagine a solution to my struggle. I couldn't even pray about it, knowing if I dared asked God to solve this one, I pictured him roaring from heaven, "Are you crazy?" Then it happened . . . the day that changed my mind.

That summer morning, I slipped out of bed to the chatter of finches and a song sparrow's four-burst imitation of the opening notes of Beethoven's Fifth. Based on the early-morning weather in my small town of Everett, I knew the temperature was likely to rise to seventy-five degrees today, which would feel hot to many of my neighbors in Washington state's Pacific Northwest. By afternoon, parents would be rushing to the parks where their children could splash in fountains, while other families would head to the blue waters of nearby Puget Sound. Or maybe they would board the ferry toward Seattle's Pike Place Market or the Ferris wheel on Pier 57. I laughed gratefully as I compared our "hot" summer days to the ones in Texas, where my daughter, Debra, lives. Texas gets so hot the corn pops on the stalk, Debra says, and based on a few summer visits I could almost believe her.

I was thinking of Debra as I scooted down the hall of my condo, eager to call her to relate another exciting God-story, visualizing her excitement before I even picked up the phone. We enjoy exchanging evidence of God's love, joyously exclaiming over each other's discoveries. God's desire to enter our lives and bless us has been so evident—quite exceptional in fact, and sharing those stories with my only daughter is a blessing all on its own, although I'd also shared a few with her two brothers.

Tugging my chenille robe tighter about me to ward off the morning chill, I sat down at the kitchen table and phoned her. She didn't disappoint me.

"Wow, Mom!" she exclaimed, hearing my new miracle story of how I had been healed instantly of glaucoma. "God is so wonderful!"

"You should have seen the confusion on my opthalmologist's face." I chuckled. "He couldn't understand it. He even showed me the previous pictures of tests showing the hemorrhages behind my eyes. All he did was shake his head in wonderment, knowing glaucoma isn't reversible."

Thirty minutes into the call, though, I felt a familiar agitation forcing me to once again grapple with my private dilemma I felt God couldn't solve—my absurd longing to share my stories of God not only with Debra or a few close friends but with my unborn descendants who would live hundreds of years from now.

I shared some of my frustration with Debra.

"Yeah," she responded, "future descendants would sure benefit from them. "That would be great if we could. It thrills me to talk about them when I get a chance. People love personal testimonies. They confirm that God still interacts with believers the way he did in Bible times."

"I know," I said. "They touch the heart and build faith—"

"Well, Mom, your testimonies have sure done that for me. Remember how your mother told you a man appeared on that deserted beach to save you from drowning when you were four years old? And how he then disappeared? And now you have this one about how baffled your ophthalmologist was when God healed your glaucoma! My favorite, though, is how God interrupted you right in the middle of your talk at church."

"Yes . . . he broke in to deliver a powerful witness that Jesus was indeed the Christ."

"Well," Debra said, "I'll certainly never forget all the faith stories you've told me."

"I'm glad they've been a blessing to you." I switched the phone to my other ear. "I've shared all my stories with you and some with your brothers. I hope they remember those and pass them on to their kids. But I suspect a few stories will be forgotten." That's when I told her about my deeper frustration.

"Too bad we can't live longer, say, a couple hundred more years—maybe as long as Methuselah. We'd be around to tell our God stories to future descendants in person."

Debra snickered. "Methuselah . . . 969 years? Nice thought, Mom. Even if you keep up your aerobics, alfalfa sprouts, and quinoa, there's no way you're ever going to live that long!"

Even though she was joking, the truth of her words struck with asteroid-like impact, reminding me of my conundrum: How could I defy the odds and live long enough to convey God's remarkable deeds to my unborn posterity? I felt I needed to be there in person to do that effectively. Not just my salvation experience, but also the moments when I received supernatural direction from the Holy Spirit, experienced healings, saw prayers answered, and even witnessed outright miracles. I knew God wasn't limited to his one act of salvation. I had encountered such profound and astonishing divine interventions.

I pictured my progeny growing up in a culture that was swiftly becoming more secular and atheistic, and less aware of God's reality. I worried that some of them in the coming decades or centuries, like many Christian youth today who are leaving the faith, might also be swayed. My testimonies would convince them God exists and could do marvelous things for them; I even imagined their voices beseeching me from the future: "Tell us—we need to hear your stories!"

Of course, some of my stories were written in my journals, but who would find them there? It seems likely my journals—and the testimonies in them—could easily disappear forever after my demise. The mere thought struck an emotional punch to my heart.

After Debra and I ended our phone call, I fixed some scrambled eggs and rushed through breakfast, anxious to get to my Bible reading. But first, as I did every morning after breakfast, I ambled to the glass door that led to my balcony. Still perplexed, I slid open the door and stepped out into the early morning coolness, breathing in the wet-scented dew clinging to the neighborhood's profusion of red and purple rhododendrons.

With my birds-eye view from the top floor of my high-rise condo, I gazed across gabled-roofs, treetops of viridian pines and thick-set oaks, their branches canopying residential streets. I turned toward the east to stare at the lavender outline of the Cascade Mountains, delighting as the sun splashed yellow-ochre rays down its peaks. Shading my eyes with one hand, I watched the sunlight dissolve the morning haze shrouding the foothills, and with finger-like streamers of gold inch across the outlying valley and into Everett's back yard.

Thanking God for the blessing of living in such a beautiful place, I stepped back inside and closed the glass door behind me.

Squeezing past the kitchen table, I dressed and plodded through the rest of my morning ritual, still thinking about the conversation with my daughter and chuckling over her Methuselah comment.

"But Lord," I said, raising my head and looking toward the ceiling, "your blessings have been so phenomenal. I can't stand to have my wonderful accounts disappear after I die." Meandering into the front room, I plopped into my La-Z-Boy recliner, picked up my Bible, and flipped the pages to where I had left off yesterday in the book of Joshua.

A few days earlier I had finished slogging through Deuteronomy, and was hoping for a good story today, but my hopes were dashed a few verses later.

For the umpteenth time, Joshua was going to rehearse Israel's history to the people—seven hundred years of it! He didn't seem to know when enough was enough. He repeated Abraham's travels, down through Isaac, Jacob, Joseph, Moses, Aaron, the Exodus, Mount Sinai, and how God brought the Israelites into the promised land.

"Good grief," I moaned. "Here we go again."

I should have been more patient with Joshua's repetitious account, but my recent readings in Exodus, Numbers, and Deuteronomy had already worn me down with their mind-numbing census of eligible soldiers and detailed descriptions of tribal duties, registration summaries, and local ordinances. Then, all those meaningless begats with names no one can pronounce and page after page of tabernacle construction details:

> Moses reared up the tabernacle . . . fastened his sockets . . . set
> up the boards thereof . . . and put in the bars thereof . . . and
> reared up his pillars.

I had just recently made it past three long chapters where Joshua listed the names of thirty-one enemy kings defeated in battle, and the lands they won "east of the Jordan . . . west of the Jordan . . . the hill country . . . the western foothills . . . the Jordan Valley . . . the mountain slopes . . . the Judean wilderness . . . the Negev," on and on ad infinitum. It was tough for me to stay awake.

My eyes glazed over as I read about Joshua reading from his handwritten list of God's current deeds, reiterating the reasons for building stone monuments, rock piles, and wood and stone altars. Why was Joshua determined to repeat so much excruciating, sleep-inducing detail? I could handle boredom in small doses, but give me a break. I slumped in disappointment. The Scriptures were supposed to inspire. Was something wrong with me?

Tempted to skip the last chapter and move on to Judges, I nevertheless persevered, thinking the story might get better.

Well, it did.

Although I was overjoyed to be reaching the end of the minutia, I felt sad when Joshua "waxed old and was stricken" and wondered how he would express his emotions when he announced, "I am now an old man . . . soon I will die, going the way of everything on earth" (Josh. 23:2, 14). I anticipated something profound, but I couldn't believe what happened next.

In typical Israelite fashion (twenty-eight long verses of it!), Joshua again rehearsed Israel's history—practically everything already delineated in Genesis, Exodus, Leviticus, Numbers, and Deuteronomy, plus earlier parts of his own record. Why? He had told them this story before.

Couldn't Joshua have summarized past events in a few paragraphs, saying something like, "People, you already know our history . . . so, here's some new stuff you need to remember?"

I couldn't understand it, but I knew there had to be a reason for the repetition since I was reading God's Word.

I had no sooner finished the last chapter when a special hindsight kicked in from the Holy Spirit, elevating my consciousness to a new high of revelatory insight. My eyes widened. It was like I could see right into Joshua's heart. Instantly I recognized the precise purpose for all the duplication and mind-numbing parts. I understood God's reason for all the repetition—even those boring begats![1]

More significantly, I grasped why God had commanded Joshua to introduce three specific strategies to reinforce Israel's history: (1) maintain a handwritten record of God's deeds, (2) repeatedly recite those deeds, along with Moses' book of laws to the people; and (3) corroborate everything God did for Israel by producing visual aids like rock piles and other wood or stone memorials that would withstand the eroding elements of time. God knew exactly what it would take to guarantee the survival of these testimonies, and his commands about creating memorials would ensure the stories of God's marvelous works would remain to influence future generations.

My thoughts leaped ahead to stories of the leaders who followed Joshua. Down through the centuries they also told and wrote stories of God's faithfulness, also erecting rock piles and establishing other memorial monuments. These three strategies guaranteed future generations would remember what God did for their forefathers. All those reminders left me with one conviction that shouted loud and clear:

God does not want testimonies of him to die out!

I marveled at the magnitude of God's well-planned agenda—a masterpiece of purpose. I could almost hear the crash of orchestral cymbals accenting his magnum opus.

Then, something else happened. The accumulative effect of the Book of Joshua, including all the boring minutia, plus my new comprehensive insight, produced a creative spark. A jubilant WOW raced through my spirit as the spark birthed a twenty-first-century update to Joshua's methods of passing on testimonies—even to those yet unborn!

Brimming with the excitement of discovery, I suddenly knew exactly how to ensure my progeny would hear my testimonies!

No, I would not outlive Methuselah to deliver them in person. Instead, I would utilize the three methods God gave to Joshua. A contemporary approach would help me establish my own creative memorials of testimonies and perpetuate them with greater assurance of their survival. The beauty of the plan was that it could be applied to children and grandchildren of all ages, whether five or fifty.

However, I needed to test the effectiveness of this new undertaking on my living family.

I could hardly wait.

CHAPTER 2
Stage 1: The Proof Is in the Pudding

We're called to be faithful,
to take those first difficult steps—and to leave the results up to God.
—Alex Harris[1]

Exploding with adrenaline, I was ready to launch stage 1 of my Joshua Project, even though anxiety knotted my insides. Could I really pull this off? Would my new undertaking prove effective?

Yet, I couldn't deny what had happened as I finished my most recent reading of the book of Joshua. The embedded Holy Spirit in God's Word had enabled a special 20/20 hindsight, revealing a purpose to what I had previously viewed as protracted and fatiguing repetitions. With my Spirit-enabled vision I could now see how all Joshua's "boring" repetitions related to God's long-range agenda— and to solving my dilemma.

God had passed his plan to Joshua, who passed it on to the Israelites—and eventually to me! The plan seemed remarkably simple: remember the stories and never forget God. In my spirit I shouted, "Absolutely!"

The creative spark grabbed me, and now I could clearly see the three stages God's plan included, plus ideas of my own:

- **Stage 1.** Gather personal faith stories and write a short, Reader's Digest version of each to hang on the front room wall.

- **Stage 2.** Write a longer, expanded version of the faith stories to pass on to descendants using modern tools.

- **Stage 3.** Create physical memorials to represent each faith story, and design them to invoke questions.

This three-pronged strategy that guaranteed survival of Israel's eyewitness accounts of God's faithfulness and remarkable deeds—would also work for me.

This new revelatory insight solved my dilemma of how to communicate my testimonies to my descendants. Using similar strategies and tapping into my imagination and creativity, I could achieve the same results using modern techniques. My testimonies could be perpetuated with greater assurance that they would reach future generations.

And in that moment, I knew this didn't apply just to me.

God's strategies would work for all Christians, enabling them to influence their living children and grandchildren in an innovative and unique way, and also preserve their personal testimonies long after their demise. Years down the line they would reach yet-unborn descendants, confirming to them what God is capable of and how far he goes to demonstrate his power for his beloved children.

The entire experience ignited a fire in my bones. I was ready to plunge into my new project.

Gathering My Material

I started by sorting through my voluminous journals and pulling out all my testimonies. Then I began recording others that I had never written down. My preliminary gathering was a laborious project, but I was amazed when I listed all these events and stories. I quickly pulled together multiple testimonies, including accounts of:

- an angel who disappeared after saving me from drowning at a deserted beach;
- as a new believer, learning the miraculous power of verbalizing the "name" of Jesus;
- the Holy Spirit warning me ahead of time when in danger of being shot by a freeway-sniper;
- an immediate healing of glaucoma by two unseen, but felt, angels;
- a visual confirmation of heaven and life after death during a memorial service;
- literal protection from a direct satanic attack;
- a voice from God sending me 1,500 miles out of my planned destination to fulfill an elderly woman's secret prayer.

And I knew my list would keep growing.

My Joshua List

After collecting these faith stories, I typed up short summaries—two or three descriptive sentences of each to hang on the wall in my front room (chapter 7 shows a picture). I called this list my Reader's Digest version (which I soon shortened to simply Digest). My goal was to incite curiosity and prompt questions from my young adult children and grandchildren when they visited. Their questions would give me the opportunity to tell them more details and engage in face-to-face conversations about those events.

I also began working on assembling the full accounts of these events so they could be printed in a special book. I knew a book like that would stand as a permanent record of God's work in my life, just like those created by Joshua and later leaders of Israel. I planned to make provisions in my will for this book to be handed down to my descendants, and had ideas for CDs, DVDs, videos, and audio recordings (see chapter 7).

The list on my front room wall ended up three feet long because God has blessed me numerous times (to date, I have forty items in my list). I titled it "My Joshua List" and opened it with an explanatory paragraph. My opening paragraphs and six examples of those items that my children and grandchildren will read when they visit me, are below. (I provide the details about these six and other testimonies in chapters 9 through 34.

MY JOSHUA LIST

"I will give thanks to the Lord with my whole heart;
I will recount all of your wonderful deeds!"
(Ps. 9:1–2)

Joshua, prior to his death and also in his farewell speech before he died (Josh. 12 and 24) kept reminding the tribes of Israel over and over again of all the specific incidents where God was with them—specifically where he gave them victory in the wars waged against their enemies, so they could possess the land God promised to them. Joshua's words were recorded. Why? So, Israel would never forget what God did for them. His hope was that it would lead them to always trust, obey and serve God. Joshua's list was to act as a reminder for not only the tribes at that time, but for future generations.

I decided to compile my own "Joshua List"—all the moments in my life where God intervened to show his grace, love and protection, so that I, too, would never forget. I am also hoping it will serve as a testimony to you, my children and grandchildren of the loving faithfulness of God. My list is long, which necessitated my not going into descriptive detail.

1934: *(4 years old) saved from drowning on a deserted beach by man who afterwards disappeared.*

1937: *(7 years old) heard voice warning me of impending danger from my estranged father*

1956: *(25 years old) God miraculously healed me overnight of tuberculosis*

1960: *(29 years old) God gave me a powerful witness that Jesus is the Christ*

1977: *God literally spoke to me, enabling my escape from Mormon Fundamentalists who held me prisoner*

1980: *God led me out of the LDS Church into the glorious kingdom of his dear Son*

Creating my Joshua List, in both the Digest version and later, the Expanded account (stage 2), took time and work. But I'm glad I didn't put it off. These written accounts of God's work in my life demonstrated for me and anyone else who saw them how faithful God had been in my life. Although I had journaled about some of these events, it would have been much harder for future generations to have found my accounts in those journals and much easier for them to have been lost altogether. With my experiences preserved in special book form, I could rest assured that my many extraordinary testimonies about God's faithfulness, especially the unique ways he showed his love to me, would not go to the grave with me. They were just too wonderful to let die.

Stage 1's Two Surprises

Before my children and grandchildren even saw my Joshua List, I discovered an unanticipated benefit—its effect on *me*. In moments of discouragement, spiritual lethargy, or doubt (we all have those moments), I found myself ambling over to my list.

As I read the abbreviated descriptions, I relived the details of each divine encounter and found my love deepening for God's abiding trustworthiness. The mere recall of these experiences increased my faith, enlivened my weary spirit, and pulled me out of any slump, reassuring me of his continued presence. Reading the list always led me to say, *"Thank you, Lord! You have always been there for me—and, you still are, even though I might not feel it sometimes."* There was no way I could doubt it.

Knowing its effect on me, I could hardly wait to see whether the Joshua list of my accounts would affect my children and grandchildren. Would it transform them in any way? The proof, as they say, is in the pudding, and my pudding turned out to be delicious!

It didn't take long before I had evidence my Joshua List was producing a significant effect on my family, and their declarations of deepened faith and renewed awareness of God thrilled me. Their reactions convinced me that my Joshua Project would have a similar influence for future descendants, who I now knew how to reach thanks to the three-staged model in the Scriptures.

To demonstrate the power of *The Joshua Project*, I include here the reactions of my daughter and two of my grandchildren after asking them to write it down.[2]

My Grandson Reacts to My Joshua List

Isaac was nineteen when he visited me from Texas and spied my Joshua List hanging on the wall. I watched him reading the list while I stood at the stove in the kitchen, heating up some soup.

He stood there for a long time perusing my stories. Finally, he pointed to the list and called to me. "Hey, Grandma, I never heard this one. And what about this one?" That was my cue. I turned off the burner, rushed (trying not to look like I was) into the front room, and invited him to sit down so I could tell him the full stories. This is how Isaac describes the experience:

> I live out of state and was visiting my grandma. I happened to see something new . . . a long list hanging on her front room wall. Curiosity got the better of me—after all, it was in plain sight and not private. Much to my surprise, it was nothing like I'd ever seen before. It was called, "My Joshua List." I read the top paragraph about Joshua and why she created it, then began skimming down the long list of events where God had intervened in her life.
>
> "Hey Grandma," I called. "What's this about . . . when you were four years old and saved from drowning in the ocean by a man who disappeared afterwards?"

"Good grief, Isaac!" she responded from the kitchen. "You mean you haven't heard the one about the angel? Take a seat." She then told me about that incident, and other stories on her list.

Throughout the years, I heard more of her wonderful testimonies about God's love, power and protection in her life. Having them spelled out on a list was great. Hearing them was even greater. Not only were they amazing in themselves, but it told me that if God did those things for her, he could do the same for me. I could never doubt God after seeing her list of testimonies and hearing her share the particulars. We live in different states, so I'm planning on each time we are together to ask her if she has another good testimony story to share. I'm sure she will.

My Granddaughter Reacts to My Joshua List

Kimberly was 29 years old when she first saw my list. She describes her thoughts about it:

> My grandmother's Joshua List is astounding. I am so thankful she made one. It is awesome for me to read the numerous encounters and miracles she received from God during her lifetime, big and small. It truly affects me, knowing these events really happened. Also, that I'm privileged to hear about them first-hand, as well as read them.
>
> It is easy to believe miraculous stories in Bible times, but deep down we sometimes think that sort of thing doesn't happen anymore. But they truly do! It's just that we don't hear them shared, or haven't had something like a Joshua List passed down to us to confirm how God is still moving. Her list reminds me of his love for me, and how real and present he is. It has also deepened my faith in God, knowing if he did those things for her, he can certainly do them for me.
>
> This led me to prepare my own Joshua List. Every time something happens where I know God was there or did something wonderful for me, I immediately record it so I can be reminded

later. Then in the future, any time I'm down or discouraged I can look at both my grandmother's Joshua List and mine, and see God's steadfast love for both me and my family throughout the years.

Kimberly surprised me after she encountered my list by creating a four-minute YouTube video, singing a song she composed about me titled, "Grandma's Song" (see endnote for the URL).[3] Her lyrics illustrate the power of sharing testimony stories with grandchildren. Her song also depicts what a godly family should be all about.

My Daughter Reacts to My Joshua List

Debra writes about her response to my Joshua List:

> I live in Texas, and my mother in Washington State. We always talk on the phone, and on one occasion she shared she had started a Joshua List of her testimonies to hang on her front room wall. She went on to briefly explain what it was.
>
> Wow, I thought, that is really cool. I didn't remember Joshua keeping a record like that, so I asked her where it was in the Bible.
>
> When we got off the phone, I immediately looked it up. Sure enough, that's exactly what Joshua did. I marveled as I read all the things he testified about on God's faithfulness. Yes, it really was like he was making a list, remembering and writing down all the mighty things God had done for Israel in the past, and also in his own lifetime.
>
> Reading about this man I never knew, who was recording the mighty works of God in his life, caused my faith in God to grow and be strengthened even more. And this is what my mom was also doing!
>
> A year later, I hopped on a plane to visit her. I looked on her front room wall, and there it was—not just a single, 8x11 sheet of paper. It was three feet long! Each itemized testimony was only two or three sentences, briefly describing experiences when God performed a miracle in her life. Her full accounts

were in a book she planned to pass down in the family, along with special objects she had created as memorial reminders.

As I started to read down the list, I stopped. "Oh Mom, I remember this one! Oh, and this one too!" I remembered them because when I was a young child growing up, she shared some of them with me. At that time, I hung on to every word. It helped me to know that because he did those things for my mom—and God loves *all* of us so much—I believed he would do the same for me.

I continued reading to the end of the list. There were some I didn't recall. "What about this one?" I asked. "And tell me about this one!" So, of course she did, and together we both praised God and rejoiced over his amazing power and love. The experiences she shared strengthened my faith in God and gave me hope, causing me to reflect on the things God had done in my own life.

I now plan to make my own "Joshua List." I want my children and others family members to know that God is alive and still moving today. Most of all, that he will do the same for them.

My mom's stories still affect me. Her life is not over yet, so I'm sure there will be many more testimonies she adds to her Joshua List. I can hardly wait!

A Crucial Confirmation

After seeing the reactions to my Joshua List, I recognized how ingenious God had been to require both verbal and written testimonies. Even if you are diligent about telling your wonderful stories of God's hand in your life, children or grandchildren are highly likely to forget important details as the years pass. This is especially true when you have shared so many.

This truth was reinforced to me when I was talking with one of my children on the telephone. I referred to a faith story I had shared years prior, and he said, "Oh, isn't that the one where you . . ." But I realized he was thinking of a different account, so then had to repeat both stories.

His misunderstanding was similar to someone saying, "Oh yes, I remember the story of when Moses led the children of Israel across the Red Sea on a special ark made from gopher wood, enabling them to sail away and escape the Egyptians. After forty days and nights, the release of a bird told them the Promised Land had been reached."

OK—so this example is a tad hyperbolized, but it demonstrates what could happen when people only hear various stories but never see a written account. To prevent your own stories from becoming similarly garbled, you need to leave a written version.

The Final Assessment

No question—the first stage of my Joshua Project worked!

Witnessing such success made me more excited than ever to continue with stage 2 (writing the Expanded version), and stage 3 (creating physical memorials to coincide with the list of my testimonies). I was now determined future descendants would receive a record of my firsthand experiences of God's love. I knew that my testimony could bolster their faith on the reality of God's presence in their own lives, which they, in turn, could pass on to their descendants.

Yes, a Joshua Project could glorify God forever!

You are probably convinced by now that *The Joshua Project* is "a nice idea." The next chapter will prove that it is so much more than that.

CHAPTER 3
God's Precise Purpose for Testimonies:
Understanding Your Reciprocal Responsibility

May I never forget the good things he does for me . . . Let all that I am
praise the LORD. Ascribe to the LORD the glory due to His name.
—Pss. 103:2 NLT; 29:2 NASB

A tidal wave of destructive plagues swept through the land of Egypt, galvanizing a mass movement of unparalleled dimensions. Thousands of Israelites were led out of bondage to trek hundreds of miles to the barren Sinai desert and seal their covenant relationship with God. The Israelites had witnessed miraculous demonstrations of God's power along the way, and those extraordinary displays were emblazoned in their minds—at least for the moment. God could already predict problems. He knew that people forget.

God's Solution

God did not want the children of Israel to forget what he had done for them, and also wanted their children and grandchildren to know about their miraculous rescue. Therefore, he placed a heavy responsibility on Israel—they must ensure that future generations would receive their eyewitness accounts.

God did not simply hope for the best but spelled out his expectations in specific terms:

> Repeat them again and again to your children. Talk about them
> when you are at home and when you are on the road, when you
> are going to bed and when you are getting up. (Deut. 6:7–8)

Writing generations later, the Psalmist makes clear that the stories of Israel's rescue had survived and that the Israelites understood exactly why God had given such instructions:

> We will not hide these truths from our children; we will tell the
> next generation about the glorious deeds of the LORD, about
> his power and his mighty wonders . . . so the next generation

might know them—even the children not yet born—and they in turn will teach their own children. So each generation should set its hope anew on God not forgetting his glorious miracles and obeying his commands. (Ps. 78:4, 6–7)

The Three-staged Survival Plan

God revealed his three specific methods—written accounts, spoken recitations, and memorial monuments—to ensure testimonies of his glorious deeds would survive generation after generation. And he included one more as an additional reinforcement: celebratory observances. Throughout the Old Testament, God commanded that his people create and practice these "memorial reminders," described as follows:

Written Accounts

God gave the task of creating reminders through written scrolls, tablets, and books mostly to the leaders. After a military victory over Amalek, God told Moses,

> Write this for a memorial in a book, and rehearse it in the ears of Joshua. (Exod. 17:14 KJV)

He issued the same command to many of his prophets. To Isa.:

> Go now, write it on a tablet for them, inscribe it on a scroll, that for the days to come it may be an everlasting witness. (Isa. 30:8 NIV)

To Jer.:

> Take again another scroll and write on it all the former words that were in the first scroll which Jehoiakim the king of Judah burned. (Jer. 36:28 KJV)

To John:

> [God] sent an angel to present this revelation to his servant John, who faithfully reported [wrote down] everything he saw. This is his report of the word of God and the testimony of Jesus Christ. (Rev. 1:1–2)

Spoken Recitations

The Israelites understood that reciting aloud the stories of God's great deeds should be the primary method to pass on their testimonies. In Deuteronomy, Moses tells the people:

> In the future, when your son asks you, "What is the meaning of
> the stipulations, decrees and laws the Lord our God has com-
> manded you?" tell him: "We were slaves of Pharaoh in Egypt,
> but the Lord brought us out of Egypt with a mighty hand.
> Before our eyes the Lord sent signs and wonders—great and
> terrible—on Egypt and Pharaoh and his whole household. But
> he brought us out from there to bring us in and give us the land
> he promised on oath to our ancestors. (Deut. 6:20–23)

God also made it clear that the written records of his deeds and his com-mands (contained in the first five books of the Bible, the Torah) should be recited to the people at the end of every seventh year during the Festival of Shelters. It was mandatory for leaders to do this. They were to preserve and perpetuate Moses' account, to keep God's name in remembrance so the people would never forget what he did for them:

> Do this, so that your children who have not known these
> instructions will hear them and will learn to fear the Lord your
> God. Do this as long as you live. (Deut. 31:13)

Reciting from the Torah was no brief presentation. It began as far back as God's calling of Abraham out of Mesopotamia, then proceeded through the accounts of Isaac, Jacob, Joseph, Moses, Aaron, the Exodus, and the giving of the law. Centuries later, Ezra the priest (who led the second expedition from Babylonia), spent seven days reading and explaining it, while the people stood and listened from "early morning until noon" each day (Neh. 8: 1–5).

Often, when leaders knew their death was imminent, the lengthy pre-sentation would be recited again, reemphasizing the importance of the commandments and reminding the people how God had protected and guided Israel through the years. Joshua told the people, "Soon I will die, going the way of everything on earth." (Josh. 23:14), so he

> summoned all the tribes of Israel to Shechem, including their
> elders, leaders, judges, and officers. So they came and presented

themselves to God. Joshua said to the people, "This is what the LORD, the God of Israel, says: Long ago your ancestors, including Terah, the father of Abraham and Nahor, lived beyond the Euphrates River, and they worshiped other gods. But I took your ancestor Abraham from the land beyond the Euphrates and led him into the land of Canaan. (Josh. 24:1–3)

Samuel also followed this familiar format when giving his farewell address:

"I stand here before you—an old, gray-haired man . . . Now stand here quietly before the Lord as I remind you of all the great things the Lord has done for you and your ancestors." (I Sam. 12:2, 7)

Celebratory Observances

As another layer to ensure that Israel's descendants would never forget how he had brought them out of Egypt, God added a celebratory commemoration to supplement written accounts and the spoken word—the Seder meal, announced with a distinctive blast of trumpets.

> On the seventh day [of the Passover celebration] you must explain to your children, "I am celebrating what the LORD did for me when I left Egypt." This annual festival will be a visible sign to you, like a mark branded on your hand or your forehead. Let it remind you always to recite this teaching of the LORD: "With a strong hand, the LORD rescued you from Egypt." So observe the decree of this festival at the appointed time each year.

> Then your children will ask, "What does this ceremony mean?" And you will reply, "It is the Passover sacrifice to the LORD, for he passed over the houses of the Israelites in Egypt. And though he struck the Egyptians, he spared our families." (Exod. 13:8–10; 12:26–27)

The memorized text, recited by the father and still practiced today, rehearses the angel of death passing over the Israelites in Egypt and their liberation from bondage. The main thrust is, "Once we were slaves, and God brought us out with a mighty hand." The intent is to make sure everyone at the table, even the youngest, remembers.

The script for the Passover meal, even thousands of years after it was initiated, calls for the continued use of first-person pronouns. "WE were slaves to Pharaoh in Egypt, and God brought US out with a strong hand." Many Jews today carry on this tradition and abide by the same script. The consistent use of such language facilitates a communal experience and intrinsic oneness with ancient Israel and God.

In addition to the Passover's Seder meal, God commanded six other feasts, those of the Unleavened Bread, First Fruits, Pentecost, Trumpets, Day of Atonement, and Tabernacles.[1] Trumpets were to be used to announce all the feasts with distinctive blasts.

Christians today have a similar observance—the Eucharist or communion. This time-honored celebratory observance reminds us of how Christ shed his blood for our deliverance.

Memorial Monuments

God decreed one more method for Israel to spread knowledge of him and testify to his remarkable works and laws. In addition to written accounts, spoken recitations, and celebratory observances, God often instructed his people to create physical monuments to mark particular events or blessings.

These physical monuments were created from wood, rocks, and other materials expected to withstand the test of time (stage 3 of our Joshua Project, the creating of memorials, is designed to do the same). These monuments were meant to keep stories alive and serve as vital visual aids for descendants who were not eyewitnesses to the Exodus or other miraculous deeds.

Israel kept God's name in remembrance forever using six diverse memorial forms as God commanded them. A variety of materials were utilized in addition to altars of wood and stone, including jewelry, grains, and trumpets. Examining these six kinds of biblical memorials demonstrates how we can create our own memorials from virtually anything.

Altars. Although we know altars were in use in other ancient religions, including in Egypt, the first altar recorded in the Bible was built by Noah (Gen. 8:20). Usually made of stone or wood, the crafting and geographical placing of these altars commemorated events such as miracles, communications from God or angels, and the establishment of covenants and promises. They were used for worship, which often involved animal sacrifices.

Rocks. Rock piles were often used to note significant events in Israel's history. For example, in Joshua 4:1–5, God directed that stones be used to create a memorial at the river Jordan to mark the time when he held back the waters so the people could cross on dry ground.

> When all the people had crossed the Jordan, the LORD said to Joshua, "Now choose twelve men, one from each tribe. Tell them, 'Take twelve stones from the very place where the priests are standing in the middle of the Jordan. Carry them out and pile them up at the place where you will camp tonight.'"

> So Joshua called together the twelve men he had chosen—one from each of the tribes of Israel. He told them, "Go into the middle of the Jordan, in front of the Ark of the LORD your God. Each of you must pick up one stone and carry it out on your shoulder—twelve stones in all, one for each of the twelve tribes of Israel."

Joshua also made sure to explain the memorial's purpose:

> We will use these stones to build a memorial. In the future your children will ask you, "What do these stones mean?" Then you can tell them, "They remind us that the Jordan River stopped flowing when the Ark of the LORD's Covenant went across." These stones will stand as a memorial among the people of Israel forever. (Josh. 4:6–7)

Jewelry. Jewelry was specified as "stones of memorial." God directed craftsmen to inscribe the names of the twelve tribes on onyx stones and set them in gold filigree upon the shoulders of the high priest's ephod (Exod. 28:12–14; 39:6–7 KJV). They served to remind the people that the high priest represented the people of Israel to God and, like God, bore their burdens on his shoulders.

Grain, oil, herbs, and food. Grain offerings, oil, and frankincense were offered up in the smoke on the tabernacle's altar "as a memorial to the Lord" (Lev. 21:3). Also, a two-quart container of manna was commanded to be kept as "a memorial" in the ark of the covenant, to remind Israel when he fed them manna in the wilderness (Exod. 16:32–34). For the table of shewbread, he said, "You shall put pure frankincense on each row that it may be a memorial portion for the bread, even an offering by fire to the Lord." (Lev. 24:7)

What Happened to All Those Memorials?

Most of ancient Israel's memorial monuments have perished. The original copies of the Law have also disappeared. However, God saw to it that copies of the scrolls were faithfully preserved by scribes, ensuring his words would pass down through the centuries. Today, we have the stories and testimonies in our Bible that give witness to God, provide us the privilege (and necessity) of understanding his spiritual truths and what he requires of us, and to help us learn about his marvelous works and promises so we know what he can also do for us.

Memorials for Our Joshua Project?

Few in our contemporary American society still build the types of memorials used by Israel. But that doesn't mean your Joshua Project should exclude such memorials. You can create and fashion a variety of impactful memorials using modern materials (directions provided in chapter 8) to tie in with your written testimonies from your Joshua List that is displayed on the wall. These memorial objects are intended for the benefit of living family members, but they can also be passed on to future generations.

Place these memorials in your home with the idea that they will invoke questions. Like Joshua said of the memorial built at the Jordan River, *"Your children and grandchildren will ask you what they mean."* When they ask questions, you will have an opportunity to share in full what the memorial represents in your walk with God.

Does God Really Hold Us to the Same Standards of Keeping Him in Remembrance?

Hebrews 13:8 tells us God is the same yesterday, today, and forever. "Same" means that today God retains his same character of old, stands for the same moral laws, continues performing remarkable acts in his children's lives, and also expects us to testify and glorify him—just as he commanded Israel. It would be unreasonable to assume that he does not want the blessings and deeds in our lifetimes to be acknowledged, verbally declared, and passed on to future generations.

The content of your remembrances will be equivalent to those created by the people of Israel. Your testimonies will also include stories of God's deliverance, salvation, healings, answered prayers, and other divine interventions. You are an eyewitness to God's work in your life. You are not retelling a second or third-hand story of what God did for someone else. God elevated this procedure of testimony with Israel, and he expects us to follow the pattern.

If we make the Lord our refuge, he has pledged to answer us and be with us in our troubles (Ps. 50:15), and give his angels charge over us to keep us in all our ways (Ps. 91:9–11). Personal testimonies should describe times when we have received that kind of help.

Don't misunderstood the purpose of *The Joshua Project*. It is not meant to take the place of reading the Scriptures. The Bible in the home takes priority—that's the main source for learning about God and his love, provisions, and expectations for us. Nevertheless, a person's faith can be reinforced through hearing personal testimonies. Your first-person witness will convince family members and your posterity that God is alive and active today just like he was in ancient Israel. Your stories provide evidence that God continues to perform blessings, such as repair a broken marriage, heal a sick child, rescue a friend from addiction, provide guidance, save from danger, answer prayer, and more.

Preserving your testimonies through written accounts, spoken recitations, and memorial monuments will accomplish the following:

- offer influence and provide a safeguard so that your children and posterity will never forget God and will remember to keep his commandments;

- act as a continual reminder that God will reach down from heaven to bless them because he promised to remain "alert and active, watching over his word to perform it [in his children's lives]." (Jer. 1:12 AMP); and

- glorify God.

Will Your Joshua Project Do Anything Special for You?

Though the focal point of your project is family and progeny, you will also be affected by this process. It will:

- bolster you in times of discouragement;

- help you remember your stories as age, or lack of telling, dims your memory; and

- bring blessings because you obeyed God's commands to glorify him through testimony passed on to your descendants.

How to Start?

Your first step (stage 1) is to make a written list of your testimonies. The abbreviated, Digest version comes first; the longer Expanded version can be started a little later (stage 2). The next step after that will be creating corresponding memorials (stage 3) that will give you opportunities to recite your full accounts when asked about them.

Don't worry if you feel like you don't have any testimonies to share. Your life isn't over. And even if you can't recall any particular event you consider miraculous or out of the ordinary, you have at least one very important testimony—your salvation experience. It was at that point, as the hymn goes, when you first saw the light, felt the burden of your heart roll away, and were redeemed from bondage and assured of eternal life. Your ultimate testimony is that God's love and forgiveness are real.

Further, if you have trouble recalling or recognizing incidents that involved God's hand, reading the personal testimonies examples contained in Part Two (chapters 9–34) of this book will:

- help you recognize the variety of ways God interjects himself into his children's lives;
- expand your spirit into a fuller recognition of God's love;
- strengthen your faith;
- enable you to recognize his willingness to make similar experiences available to you;
- accelerate your prayer life; and
- enhance your relationship with Christ.

Our Motivation and the Biblical Imperative

God made the promulgation of testimonies an imperative, meaning an urgent matter requiring immediate action. Israel repeatedly experienced negative consequences when they succumbed to the false gods of the times and stopped telling the stories of God's deliverance. It took various reformers, such as the judges, Hezekiah, Josiah, and Nehemiah, reciting the written record and its testimonies, and telling the miraculous stories related to their memorials, to bring the Israelite people back to God.

Similar consequences could befall our children due to the influence of today's false ideologies. But our testimonies can act like "reformers" to call them back to God. Therefore, I challenge you to wrestle with these probing questions: "Do I feel this need strong enough to pursue God's imperative? If not, why not? What am I lacking?"

Without motivation, your Joshua Project can fall by the wayside unfinished and your testimonies lost forever. The right motivation causes us to act despite obstacles. Unfortunately, motivation levels vary with each individual. So, how do you acquire the required level?

For some, simply comprehending God's mandate in the Scriptures to perpetuate testimonies may be enough motivation. Others, even if cognizant of God's command, may find themselves wondering whether such a project is really necessary. They may argue, "If we teach our children and grandchildren the Bible when they are young and send them to church, that should be enough. Why should they be any more at risk if they don't hear our testimonies?"

Those people can only find the necessary motivation when they understand why our descendants are at risk and what might happen to them if a Joshua Project is not pursued. Modern societal influences are proving just as spiritually damaging as the ideology of the false gods that enticed the ancient Israelites. While you as a parent or grandparent may be somewhat aware of today's secular influences, it is essential that you become more informed about the destructive power of today's postmodern culture and its determined agenda.

Today's Anti-God Agenda

Postmodernism's insidious ideologies, backed by militant atheists, secular humanists, and radical leftists, are permeating our society and schools, undermining absolute truth, and tearing apart the moral fabric of America. The America of long ago "has disappeared," states Dr. Michael Youssef in his 2018 book, *The Hidden Enemy*. It has been "replaced by . . . a secularist America . . . [where] children and grandchildren are growing up in a very different America . . . that no longer values biblical principles and moralities."[2]

The individuals and organizations behind today's secular ideologies have one goal: to diminish organized religion and eliminate the biblical God and his moral and ethical absolutes. They promote the idea that only liberation from God and the demands and restrictions of the Bible enables individuals to more easily reach their human potential.

Using intellectual and syllogistic reasoning and logic, these philosophies are seducing young people into a godless worldview. Too many now believe faith in a God is "far-fetched," similar to believing in "the Easter bunny."[3] "If God is real," many youth and young adults are now demanding, "give us proof!"

Unfortunately, pointing them to a Bible written thousands of years ago may not seem like proof to these young skeptics. They are convinced by louder and stronger voices that say the Bible is full of fables, and the Scriptures contradict science.[4]

Do not, for one minute, believe your beloved children, teens, and young adults are immune to these pressures. The powers-that-be are exerting a devastating influence, and many are succumbing, including teens in Christian homes and young adults with Christian upbringing.

Out of the 70 million US youth in Generation Z, only one in eleven teens is an "engaged Christian," according to LifeWay Research, cited in Josh McDowell's book *The Last Christian Generation*. Teens are abandoning the church after high school graduation, with 63 percent not believing Jesus is the son of God, 51 percent viewing Jesus' resurrection from the dead as a myth, and 68 percent disregarding the Holy Spirit's reality.[5] While some may return to the faith of their parents, 69 percent will remain gone.

Becoming more knowledgeable about the seductive power of this spiritually damaging movement and the concentrated effort of those behind it will show you why your children and grandchildren can be at risk despite a Christian upbringing.

A Joshua Project containing the declaration of your modern-day witness of God's reality and love has the power to bring your children and grandchildren—and even your unborn descendants—back to the Bible. Or bring them there for the first time.

Your spiritual stories have power, and can play a crucial role in the lives of both living and future descendants whose faith may be hanging like a thread. Your testimony can help them restore and maintain Christian beliefs, draw them back to the Bible, and persuade them that the true God of the Bible not only still exists, but is waiting with wide-open arms to receive them.

You may be considering which faith stories to include in your Joshua Project, or you may be wondering if you have any stories to tell. In the next chapter, we will examine at least thirteen kinds of stories that are worthy of your testimony.

CHAPTER 4

The Sharing of Testimonies
Defining Miracles, Answered Prayers, and
Other Divine Encounters

I am the LORD, the God of all the peoples of the world.
Is anything too hard for me?

—Jer. 32:27

"I can't believe what just happened . . . it's a miracle!"

I shouted this in amazement when I received an on-the-spot healing at a Christian meeting in the pine-covered mountains of Parowan, Utah in the summer of 1980. Until that moment, I had been facing a radical surgery to completely remove my paralyzed colon (for the full story, see chapter 19, "Miracle in the Mountains").

God has given me three healing miracles in my lifetime. In addition to the colon, I was healed overnight of tuberculosis (chapter 11) and instantly cured of glaucoma (chapter 25). I have also received a variety of less dramatic blessings over the years—those day-to-day, tranquil kind that gently descend upon us when God responds to our needs in other ways.

God doesn't always choose the route of sensational miracles. He can bless through answered prayers, premonitions of danger, directions to a lost item, help from an angel in disguise, subtle nudges from the Holy Spirit, and numerous other methods. Such blessings may not inspire as much excitement as a dramatic healing, but these gifts from God should be considered worthy of testimony even if not as flashy. Describing them can still deliver a spiritual impact. So, it is important not to overlook any in your Joshua Project. It can easily happen.

Through the years, some of these incidents may have slipped into the recesses of your mind, tucked far away. You may also have experiences you are not sure how to categorize—was that from God or was it just happenstance?

This chapter will help you recognize God's hand in your life and help you remember incidents you might not have thought about in years. Reading the testimonies in chapters 9 through 34 will also provide clarity and confirmation about what you have received.

God can bless in many ways, and many of those are described in the lists in the next few pages. Yet these lists are not exhaustive. They can't be. Individuals face unique life circumstances, and God selects a variety of ways to bring his plans to fruition. It would be impossible to list every tool used by God.

God addresses three objectives when he performs miracles or intervenes in our lives in less dramatic ways:

- He wants to bless his children because his intrinsic nature is love.

- He wants to reveal himself and his nature.

- He wants to produce faith stories we can share to empower others, particularly our family members.

Stories about supernatural acts of God attract attention. Children and grandchildren will often ask for them to be repeated; teenagers will remember them; and young adults remain influenced by them, especially when they are attacked by doubts or cultural pressures of atheism. When confronted, they recall your stories and it makes them think, "What others are saying sounds logical. But God has to be real. I can't dismiss that powerful testimony Grandma shared with me."

God's Variety of Blessings

A beloved hymn came to mind as I prepared to write about the various ways God blesses: "Count Your Many Blessings, Name Them One by One." I felt the need to do exactly that. Separate, one by one, all his different *kinds* of miraculous acts into specific categories for the sake of conciseness.

Miracles—those sensational healings that defy the medical world—were easy to categorize. But when I tried to pigeonhole other types of blessings, I ended up with too many. To simplify matters, I settled for two categories: "miracles" and "divine encounters."

- **Miracles.** These blessings are typically more immediately spectacular, such as instant healings that defy natural law—deaf ears and blind eyes opened, crippled bodies straightened, life restored after a clinical declaration of death, and other extraordinary feats.

- **Divine encounters.** These less dramatic experiences can include receiving a strong, inner certainty about the outcome of a concern; experiencing God's calming presence during tragedy that passes understanding; feeling a flooding experience of his love; perceiving a quiet whisper of direction from the Holy Spirit; hearing God's voice; discerning warnings of imminent danger; getting help from an angel in human form; and more. Your personal salvation experience also belongs in this category. Your Joshua Project will most likely contain more entries from this category.

Now, let's take a more in-depth look at each type.

Miracles

Dramatic miracles draw flocks of Christians (and non-Christians) to special meetings where they hope to see deeds that mystify the medical world and violate physical and scientific laws. There is no question these kinds of miracles happen. Are they real? Seventy-four percent of U.S. physicians believe in them, with 55 percent of doctors claiming to have personally witnessed one or more.[1] In an AARP survey, 37 percent of laypeople said they had witnessed miracle healings, and 42 percent claimed to have received one.[2] Sixty-six percent of Americans in general believe in miracles, and 68 percent (80 percent in some surveys) believe in them enough to pray for others to be healed supernaturally.[3]

The Definition of Miracles

C. S. Lewis gave a fine definition of miracles as "an interference with Nature by supernatural power," further explaining them as "impossible events" that break established patterns and are so "overwhelmingly improbable," we would never conceive of them being broken.[4]

Great thinkers through the centuries have labored over definitions of miracles, and I don't agree with what all of them have come up with. For example, I differ with Saint Augustine, who said, "Miracles are not in contradiction to nature. They are only in contradiction with what we know of nature." He suggested that the more science discovers more about nature, the less we will label our experiences as miracles.

I oppose his definition because miracles have nothing to do with this earth's laws of nature, discovered or undiscovered. God is an immortal "spirit" (John 4:24), and he operates outside our world of nature, utilizing higher spiritual laws unique to his makeup and environment. These laws are the primary basis for all creation and are more powerful than ours. As Creator, God can interrupt, override, and countermand a condition so that natural laws of mortality must obey. That's why we call them *super*natural.

No matter how hard we attempt to define or understand these higher laws, we will never comprehend how God operates in his sphere of pure spirit. Romans 11:34 says it is impossible to know the mind of God. This answer satisfies most Christians.

But many struggle with this question: Why does God give miracles to some but seems to withhold them from others? When this happens Christians can begin to doubt their relationship with God. "Why didn't I receive the miracle I asked for when so-and-so got one?"

The Unpredictability of Miracles

When God bestows a miracle on someone else, but not on us, it may be hard to deal with. It can cause faith to waver, especially if you have prayed fervently but God hasn't delivered you from a discouraging situation or enacted a miracle to cure your chronic ailment. Some Christians are able to work through this; some aren't. While there is no blanket answer, it can be comforting to know that biblical figures grappled with the same dilemma.

The Apostle Paul received miraculous visions, saw the resurrected Christ on the road to Damascus, and was caught up to the third heaven where he heard things beyond his ability to put into words (2 Cor. 12:2). Paul was clearly favored, called by God, and had unquestionable faith. But it didn't mean God miraculously intervened for him in every situation.

In his letter to the Corinthians, Paul describes how he asked God three times to remove his "thorn in the flesh" but notes that God chose otherwise (2 Cor. 12:7–8). We might assume that this mighty man of faith went on his merry way without disappointment or confusion. But he was human, and he wanted to know why God ignored his request. Paul had to personally work through this frustration and seek a satisfying reason. He knew a person could endure any trial (he had suffered many times) if there is an explanation.

Paul began to conclude the thorn was probably meant to humble him, to prevent his becoming proud and boastful in view of the many revelations he received. But when Christ told him, "My grace is all you need. My power works best in weakness" (2 Cor. 12:9), he achieved an even greater understanding.

Christ's presence in Paul (which he passionately wanted) could only become apparent by functioning in his weakness—not when he was strong and capable in himself.

Although Paul learned why his thorn wasn't removed, we don't always get that kind of clarity. Yet, if we know that even the Apostle Paul wasn't delivered from everything, how can we feel slighted? Like Paul, we must persevere through suffering, and we can be sure we will have Christ's presence to empower us.

It is okay to seek possible purposes for God's lack of response. But if we can't figure it out, we must accept that we may not understand the reason until later, if ever. Yet, sometimes God surprises us and may intervene at a later time. Everything hinges on God's timing.

God's Timetable

So far, no one has figured out the rationale of God's timetable. Author and speaker James Watkins, nails it down in an article titled "God is never late—but he sure is slow." Watkins points out that "God usually ignores our human deadlines . . . but real faith grows between the deadline and the deliverance."[5]

The following is from a woman who suffered debilitating back pain. She prayed about it for a long time, wondering why God hadn't come through:

> The pain was night and day, but unbearable at night. It was to the point I was getting no sleep. This made me so tired during the day, I was unable to function. Discouraged, and at my lowest point, I was on the verge of resigning as teacher of a Bible class. Continuing to pray, I told God I could deal with the lesser intensity of the pain during the day, but why couldn't he at least take away the horrible pain at night?
>
> One afternoon I lay on my bed, hoping to nap and catch up on lost sleep, when the room suddenly filled with the presence of a beautiful floral fragrance. Having experienced this fragrance in times past, I knew angels were present (see chapter 20). At that second, I didn't know why they were there. I just enjoyed knowing so. But I found out that very night.
>
> God finally gave me what I had prayed for. That night was the first time in months I was able to sleep without *any* pain, and the nighttime relief continued from that night on. Then, very gradually, the daytime pain also went away.

Why did God wait so long? What criteria does he set up that determines when he will act? I may never know, unless the long wait was to test my faith. Or, was it because others, who I knew were praying for me, had more faith than I, and it was their prayers that moved God? Nevertheless, it taught me not to complain, and "be still in the presence of the Lord, and wait patiently for him to act." (Ps. 37:7)

When wrestling with a problem that God does not seem to address right away, we need to recognize that he does bestow miracles. We know that he does because he promised he would, but acts in his own timing.

And we are confident that he hears us whenever we ask for anything that pleases him. And since we know he hears us when we make our requests, we also know that he will give us what we ask for. (1 John 5:14–15)

We also need to be reassured that since he has forgiven us through Christ, our past sins are not the reason he's holding back any healing or special deliverance:

O Lord, I call for your help . . . Pay attention to my prayer. Lord, if you kept a record of our sins, who, O Lord, could ever survive? But you offer forgiveness, that we might learn to fear you. I am counting on the Lord; yes, I am counting on him. I have put my hope in his word. (Ps. 130:5)

How God measures his timetable remains a mystery to us. Our responsibility is to continue to believe in him, walk by faith, and never let our circumstances shake our faith.

I wait quietly before God, for my victory comes from him. He alone is my rock and my salvation, my fortress where I will never be shaken." (Ps. 62:1)

Situations When God Gives Miracles

Below is my limited summation of situations and reasons for God's miracles— why they might be given and why they sometimes are withheld.

Miracles are given:

- by the grace of God, and for reasons known only to him;
- according to his timetable;
- to promote needed faith in him at a crucial life moment; and
- to spare and preserve an individual for a future calling.

Miracles may be withheld:

- to keep us humble;
- to allow us to see that God is sufficient when we call upon him in our weakness;
- to determine whether our faith in him will continue; whether we will say with Job, "Though he slay me, yet will I trust him" (Job 13:15 KJV);
- to promote insight from the experience; and
- to allow us to use our adverse experiences as preparation for ministering to others.

It is important to understand that God knows that not everyone requires a spectacular miracle. One can live a faith-filled life and have a close, amazing walk with Christ and never experience a dramatic miracle or explicit divine encounter. Trusting God to silently lead without expecting to receive miraculous interventions means you are strong enough to walk by faith, not sight (2 Cor. 5:7).

Now, we are ready to look at God's other type of blessings.

Divine Encounters

Divine encounters are often, but not always, received during prayer time. Below is a limited list of some ways you might experience a divine encounter. (I have placed asterisks by the types of encounters I feel should not be shared in a testimony meeting, although you may occasionally find a particular time to comfortably do so.) A divine encounter could be described as:

- precognitive warnings about imminent danger;
- supernatural protection during actual danger;
- a special salvation experience;

- prophetically revealed future events;*
- a natural circumstance in life that works to answer a prayer;
- being led by the Holy-Spirit to someone, or having the Holy Spirit lead someone to you;
- hearing the Holy Spirit's audible voice internally;
- hearing God's audible voice externally (described later in this book);*
- receiving the solution to a seemingly unsolvable problem;
- being directed to a lost item;
- seeing an angel, or being ministered to by one or more;*
- getting help from an angel in human form who disappears afterward; and
- experiencing an open vision, special dream, or revelation.*

God Gets to Choose

God knows whether a miracle or a divine encounter will work best for each individual. He may answer one person's prayer in a roundabout fashion through controlled circumstances while performing a direct miracle as an answer to another person's prayer. He may send an angel in an extraordinary vision to one but an angel in human disguise (or someone you know) to another. You may hear God speak a distinct sentence through the Holy Spirit within your mind, or you may hear a powerful voice external to you.

There are also times when God arranges events for our good so naturally that we may be unaware he moved at all. Often, we don't recognize his hand in our affairs until years later through hindsight. His unseen, and sometimes unnoticed, presence in our life bears out Rom. 8:28:

> And we know that God causes everything to work together for the good of those who love God and are called according to his purpose for them.

Whichever way God chooses to bless, he never holds back. He always provides help and direction when asked and responds in his own timing.

> The Lord your God will personally go ahead of you. He will neither fail you nor abandon you." (Deut. 31:6)

Paul reminds us that we are called to walk by faith, not by sight (2 Cor. 5:7). Yet many Christians yearn for a miraculous event, such as being caught up to heaven, receiving a vision, or being visited by an angel. Even many mature and devoted believers feel this natural inclination, although they are reluctant to admit it for fear of being wrongly judged as immature.

Their longing is not necessarily due to a frivolous desire to feed on the sensational. Neither does it always grow from a need to have their faith strengthened by God giving them something to "see." Rather, it can be attributed to one's earnest love and longing for God and the innate desire to experience heaven now rather than later. This is normal, and Christians should not feel wrong to feel these desires.

No Guarantees

Some Christians want to be assured they can receive a miraculous visitation just by asking for one. But we already understand that we receive things by grace, and that God is under no obligation to perform anything. Asking for a visitation does not mean you have ruined your chance for one; however, most Christians who have received miraculous experiences such as a vision of heaven or visitation by an angel, usually say they came as a surprise, not as a response to a request. The author knows of one such example.

A woman had spent two full days desperately praying nonstop for help concerning an impediment in a new ministry situation, when she was ministered to by two angelic beings (see chapter 21). Following that, she heard the external voice of God. But because this is rare, like others, she was completely surprised by what God gave her and by the manner in which it came. According to others who have heard God's voice external to themselves (explained more fully later), the encounter is so rare that it may happen only once or twice in a lifetime.

So, yes, we may receive these types of experiences, but not necessarily because we put our order in for one. God has the final word. We must continue in faith, knowing God is aware of our situation, loves us, and supports us.

They Are No Measures of Spiritual Superiority

Miracles and divine encounters are not given based on a person's individual worthiness. And dramatic manifestations do not indicate an elevation in status over those who receive the less dramatic type or those who receive nothing. All should be content to walk by faith alone.

What, then, is the major purpose for giving miracles and divine encounters? Though we know he gives them because he loves us and for other reasons listed earlier in this chapter, God does have another reason that may surprise you.

God's Gifts Are Not Always About Us

God provided manna and quail to the complaining children of Israel in the desert. Certainly not because they deserved it. He provided in this miraculous fashion to *identify* himself as the one who brought them out of Egypt and into the desert (not Moses, whom they were blaming). He also wanted to reveal two of his fundamental characteristics—his compassion and ability to provide.

Whenever God bestows blessings—whether to those who don't deserve it or those who do—he is always revealing himself. He didn't part the Red Sea only to save the Israelites, but also to communicate himself. Whether a miracle, divine encounter, manna, quail, or whatever, receiving a miraculous or divine encounter is not always about us. God may simply be impressing his identity upon you to demonstrate what he is capable of providing.

When we are a recipient, it is our responsibility to testify about what we receive and be sure to give credit where credit is due. That is, acknowledge God as the source and provider of the blessing or manifestation—especially in today's world that is intent on silencing his reality.

Your Next Step

By now, you understand the difference between miracles and divine encounters. And you recognize the importance of sharing your testimonies of God with children and grandchildren by posting a short summary, a Digest version, of your testimonies in your home, and later writing the Expanded version. Chapter 7 will provide more instructions on how to create the Digest and Expanded versions, and Chapter 8 will show you how to create memorial objects as visual aids to coincide with your faith stories. Creating all three will prove exciting and rewarding.

But there is one last consideration that must be addressed first—a singular characteristic about ourselves that needs attentive scrutiny, but remains hidden. You may have never consciously considered this aspect of sharing your faith stories, but it will impact, positively or negatively, any potential influence you intend your testimonies to have on others.

To bring this hidden property to the surface, you will encounter a critical question in the next chapter that will compel a deep self-inquiry. (I mean, *really* deep). The result may unnerve you, but you will also read about my own shameful struggle when I faced the same question, and the trauma I went through to resolve it.

Your thoughtful consideration of the next chapter's probing contents will test your character, heart, and spirituality. It will reveal your "true" self, perhaps for the first time.

Are you ready?

CHAPTER 5
Magnifying Hidden Motives: A Moment of Truth

Those who wish to boast should boast in this alone: that they truly know me and
understand that I am the Lord who demonstrates unfailing love.
—Jer. 9:24

Have you ever had a bullring "moment of truth?" Have you ever faced that critical and decisive instant when character and courage are put to the ultimate test and, forced to choose between two options, you must dig down deep inside yourself and decide which is the more pressing imperative in a current situation?

No matter what situation you face, your choice will be influenced by a powerful, self-serving motive intrinsic to human nature. Acknowledging this reality can hurl us into a moment of truth we may prefer not to face.

In the bullring, a matador responds openly to the instinct that most Christians want to avoid. He's on the stage and in the limelight, and his one primary motivation is to exalt his image. His goal is to win the adulation of the crowd by gathering shouts of *olé!* and *bravo!* It's his job.

But then comes the matador's "moment of truth" when he must decide between two choices. Does he thrust in the sword and kill the bull or let the animal live? He makes his decision by choosing which one will bring the most praise from the crowd and exalt his image. Then, victorious, he struts around the ring to the rousing roar of spectators, blaring trumpets, and tossing of flowers.

Like the matador, we may make choices based on which action will exalt our image and maintain the adoration of peers on our brief stage of life. While the matador chooses pomp and peacocking because his job demands it, we may choose this path unconsciously. It can indeed be a moment of truth when Christians are forced to acknowledge their own internal drive to receive personal adulation. Understanding this instinct helps us loosen its grip; also, realize how it affects the giving of our testimonies.

Our Self-serving Instinct

This cloaked instinct to promote ourselves in the eyes of others lies deep within most of us, suppressed. It is part of the God-given, self-preservation impulse in our physiology that compels us to save our life when danger threatens. Similarly, it applies when our self-image is at stake, compelling us to save it at all costs. To achieve this, our base instinct sways us to make the choice that will keep us in the best light before others. It may involve hiding a known secret, even lying. The following situations illustrate this instinct:

> I falsified my academic background to gain more prestige. But if I admit to it, I'll lose the limelight and adoration of colleagues.

> I'm involved in an immoral situation that if revealed would tarnish my reputation. Do I continue living a lie to save my standing in church, or tell the truth and face shame?

We want others to think we're perfect and flawless, free of any blemishes or defects. Our need to preserve our self-image is so strong that we imagine we have no serious faults or wrong motivations. Certain that all our motives are noble and Christ-like, we even cover up their true nature to ourselves . . . to the point where we believe they don't exist. Therefore, we measure our character and spirituality with a unique tape measure like the one Mary Poppins described: "Mary Poppins, practically perfect in every way."

Hellooo Down There!

If the subterranean depths of our thoughts, emotions, and motives were truly revealed to us, we would be shocked at what lies hidden to us. Shrouded in the cavernous recesses of our unconscious lie our instinctive, egotistic motives. They are so well concealed that we have no idea something bad lurks there. We strut through the many stages of our life, unaware of the hidden motives that unconsciously dictate our behavior.

For example, we may convince ourselves that our motivation for telling our faith stories is indeed God-centered. Yet, a disturbing feeling may creep in and reveal a moment of truth when we realize that underlying our desire to share our stories was a self-seeking desire to be in the limelight, to exalt ourselves— the real reason why we wanted to share our testimony in the first place. This may be hard to accept, but read on.

Self-seeking Motives and Our Testimonies

Concealed egotistic motives can influence the giving of our testimonies. We may remain unaware of this motive until someone points it out to us, we discover it through self-examination, or God reveals it to us.

Socrates said, "The unexamined life is not worth living." The Apostle Paul similarly told Christians to "examine yourselves" (2 Cor. 13:5). Only by examining ourselves can we be sure that we are motivated to share our faith stories for the right reasons.

The goal of testimonies is to strengthen the faith of others and proclaim the goodness, faithfulness, mercy and love, of Almighty God. It takes some deep digging to truly discern our underlying motives for sharing our faith stories.

By considering the following six motives, they can help uncover your unperceived rationales. You will probably deny all six at first, but do some intensive soul-searching and be totally honest. Don't rush. Mull over each item for a while.

Ask yourself, do I want to share God's marvelous acts of blessings to me because:

- I want my neat stories to be known and entertaining?
- I want people to see how God has favored me?
- I want to promote myself in the eyes of others because I enjoy the spotlight?
- Sharing makes me feel important?
- I want to show how spiritual and worthy I am to have received these blessings?
- My testimony stories are more spectacular than others' stories?

Our normal reaction is to say, "Of course, those aren't my reasons!" Naturally, we want to think our sole focus is on glorifying God. But we may find that deep down one (or more) of the six explains our real motives. One Christian, after perusing the list above, was willing to make such an admission:

> In sharing my testimonies to family, but especially in church, I always believed my motive was to truly glorify God. But, upon sober reflection, I am experiencing an unsettling feeling that maybe I do want to glorify myself—show everyone how

special God must think I am to have given me such a remarkable blessing. The self-analysis was not easy . . . actually, unpleasant. It's hard to acknowledge a side of yourself that contradicts what you have envisioned for so long.

The Need for an Absolute Focus on God

The lack of an authentic, God-centered motive in our testimonies, even if it is unconsciously neglected, hinders the effectiveness. We don't have to say something like, "Look what God did for me; I'm so special," for others to sense the missing ingredient. They may not be able to put their finger on exactly what is missing, yet the absence of a focus on God's glorification may mean your words won't convince listeners of God's reality and love. Instead, hearers may end up thinking, "Wow, look at the wonderful thing that happened to *her!*" That should not be your objective.

If you begin probing to detect your inner motives, be prepared to face some unpleasant realities about yourself. You may face a "moment of truth" like no other. Such encounters aren't pretty. I know, because it happened to me, and it was soul-wrenching.

My Experience

After I realized the truth about my true nature, I felt I could *never, ever* let anyone know what I found out. Who wants to show the whole world how defective they are? But now, fifty years later, I don't mind sharing the analysis I pursued or the answers I received because I want you to have a first-hand experience of someone who went through the process. My experience shows that any of us can be fooled about our motives, and it illustrates how the human mind works when it wants to defend itself.

I probably went further than most in trying to figure what was really inside me. Like Captain Kirk, I decided to boldly go where I had never gone before . . . to explore the strange new world of what is inside the human soul—more specifically, mine. There was only one way to do it: I asked God to show me my true self—my honest-to-goodness, unvarnished, no-holds-barred, nature—the real me.

I had no idea what I was getting into. The revelation that came was a tough pill to swallow and left me totally devastated.

Journey to the Center of My Soul

A little background is necessary to set the stage. Back in the seventies, I was a member of the Church of Jesus Christ of Latter-day Saints, often called the Mormon church. But I was familiar with Scripture and loved the Jesus of my childhood, having been raised in the Methodist Church until I was fourteen. Similar to David, who was "a man after God's own heart" but deterred by his human flaws, I sought God's heart, deterred by the flawed Mormon structure.

During those years, it was not unusual for the bishop and his counselors to visit me in the home and ask for a donation when church projects needed money. They knew my husband had left me well off. It was nothing for me to write thousand-dollar checks and hand them to these church leaders, which was a great deal of money in that time period. I felt happy I could help, believing my actions were for God because I adored him. No one could have convinced me I had any motive other than my love for God. *Absolutely no one!*

Months sailed by, and I forgot about the donations. During that time, my personal focus was on making myself perfect before God, based on Jesus' admonition in Matt. 5:48, "Be ye perfect, even as your Father in heaven is perfect." I analyzed every bit of my character, my relationship with him, my prayer life, tithing, avoidance of sin, good works, etc., weeding out all perceived negatives. Along with my attempt to achieve a self-acquired spiritual perfection, I concentrated on improving my intellectual knowledge—theology, science, astronomy, physics—because it was supposed to give me an advantage in the next world according to Mormon theology.

But, one day, in my energetic attempts for perfection, I found myself pondering. Could it be possible there was a deep-down, inaccessible level somewhere inside my spirit and soul that contains who and what I really am? Some aspect far different from how I view myself that I need to work on? After all, I was aware I couldn't hop inside me and view the subterranean depths of my inner self. I puzzled over this.

The Answer Drops into My Lap

Elated, I discovered Saint Augustine had also inquired about this. In his Confessions, he confirmed the impossibility of seeing into the depths of our own nature, referring to 1 Cor. 2:11:

Although no man knoweth the things of a man, but the spirit of a man which is in him, yet is there something of man which neither the spirit of man that is in him, itself, knoweth.[1]

To my delight, Augustine arrived at the answer the only way it could be done. Recognizing he didn't have enough of his own light to shine upon his insides and ferret out imperfections, he discerned it could only be revealed by "God's shining."

But thou, Lord, knowest all of him, who has made him . . . what I do know of myself, I [only] know by Thy shining upon me.

I grabbed hold of that. First Cor. 4:5 also states that only God can "bring our darkest secrets to light and . . . reveal our private motives."

Therefore, in spite of being practically perfect by my Mary Poppins' measuring tape, I accepted the fact I couldn't access my own insides. I would have to ask God to provide his "shining" to reveal the part I couldn't see. Certainly, whatever minor thing he showed me couldn't be too bad. Nothing big. Already having a starry-eyed image of myself, I thought that once God revealed this flaw, I could easily correct it. I grew excited as I thought about making myself really perfect for him!

So, I planned to boldly go where Augustine went, and presented my quest before God. Day after day, I relentlessly hammered at the gates of heaven. "Show me my real insides!" I also, reminded the Lord of David's valid plea:

"Search me, O God, and know my heart . . . point out anything in me that offends you, and lead me along the path of everlasting life." (Ps. 139:23)

I waited and waited. Nothing. Why was he holding back?

The Kind-hearted Grace of God

I now suspect the Lord didn't answer my prayer right away to spare me the devastating truth of how fundamentally flawed I am.

Nevertheless, due to my white-knuckled persistence, he finally showed me. What he revealed sent a paralyzing shockwave through me. The revelation came to me during the night. (Those who have experienced dreams from the Lord know the difference between God-dreams, pizza-dreams, and plain ol' human dreams. This was definitely from God.)

First, God visually showed me enlarged pictures of all the thousand-dollar checks I had given to the church (he wanted to be sure I saw them). Then, sparing nothing (after all, I asked for it), he took me down into the very depths and interior of my being to expose my true motive in giving those checks.

It was a literal plunge into total darkness. The experience is difficult to describe, except to say it was comparable to descending in an elevator in the pitch-black . . . all the way down to the rock-bottom, cavernous darkness inside of myself. And there, I visually saw it!

Through that vivid and shocking experience, God revealed my true self. My motive for donations were not for his glory at all—but for self-glorification! I wanted to exalt myself in the church's eyes, to show how wonderful I was for making such great contributions. My giving wasn't pure at all. I was also shown my unconscious deceit in covering it up so completely that I wasn't even aware of my motive.

Consciously, I had no idea of my need to glorify myself, but God's "shining" revealed the ugly truth. His luminous shining in that dark abyss inside me affirmed that my deep-down human nature was defective. Nowhere close to his standard of perfection.

To say I was crushed is putting it mildly. The devastation cut through me like a two-edged sword, splitting asunder the very core of my being. It wrenched my heart until I thought it would break.

"Nothing is more intolerable," Beethoven is reported to have said, "than admitting to one's own errors." But this was more than intolerable and more than an error. I now knew that I had a blemished soul. I was self-centered with inborn shortcomings and deficiencies, most of which I had unconsciously covered up. It was excruciating.

In the weeks following, I agonized. What other narcissistic tendencies did I have? I sensed there were other deficits he mercifully didn't reveal. What else was buried in my unconscious depths that God magnanimously and compassionately did not show me? And where did that awful self-seeking motive inside me come from in the first place? This revelation created a new set of problems for me.

If my true motives were hidden so deep only God could see them, how could I know what to work on? Further, why did Jesus admonish us to become perfect like his Father in Heaven if I have no chance of achieving that status? I also had no idea what other defects might lie deep inside me.

Loving God, I wanted to be unblemished and holy before him and be with him in heaven after death. But the revelation showed me I was helpless to redeem my abject, egocentric, prideful nature, nor could I delete other hidden defects that were intrinsic to my nature. I was too flawed. This frustrated me to no end. There had to be a solution.

I would find the answer a few years later, when I left the LDS Church. But why did it take so long? A. B. Simpson hit the nail on the head:

> We often ask the question, "why didn't God help me sooner?"
> It is not his order. He must first adjust us to the situation and
> cause us to learn our lesson from it.[2]

Discovering the Remedy

After I became a Christian, I subsequently comprehended mankind's sinful inclinations to a greater degree. I then understood that everyone was born that way—which, in a way, was comforting. But my next discovery was the best.

I learned that God had the power to rectify my hopeless condition. In fact, he had always planned to do just that. He sent Jesus to pay the price for my sinful tendencies inherited in my fallen state. Through accepting him and what he did, God's Holy Spirit and the Savior's righteousness were imputed into me. This freed me from sin's control (Rom. 4:6, 11, 24 KJV). What a wonderful shock to find out "there is no [longer] condemnation for those who belong to Christ Jesus" (Rom. 8:1).

This was huge! I was no longer condemned, even though God knew my deep-down insides. It was a miracle above all miracles. Now, I have great joy in giving, and it is authentic.

From the Psalms, Asaph's words spoke to me:

> He brought [me] to the border of his holy land . . . He cared for
> [me] with a true heart and led [me] with skillful hands . . . Now
> [he said] I will take the load from your shoulders; I will free
> your hands from their heavy tasks. You cried to me in trouble
> and I saved you. (Ps. 78:54, 72; 81:6–7)

The Challenge

I don't recommend that everyone follow my method, especially if they are not prepared to face the reality of that much truth. But your mission—should you decide to accept it—is to personally analyze at some level your inner motives when sharing what God has done for you. This is essential when testifying at church or to others because your motivation will make a difference in how you tell your godly encounters; also, for how you write your faith stories for your Joshua Project.

We need to make sure the intent for our testimonies is genuine and that we want to solely glorify him, not ourselves. Our faith stories must relay to others God's goodness, grace, mercy, love, and his ever-ready help for his children in times of need. When we acquire genuine intent, it will be evident in both our verbalized and written accounts. This will touch others at the heart-level God intends.

So, take a somewhat deep dive and, with the help of the Holy Spirit, go back to the six questions about your motives. Your honest endeavor may reveal much. It will change you and also affect the faith of future generations with greater impact.

Motives and Memory

Having stressed the importance of examining your motives before beginning your Joshua Project, it is also important not to delay. Even with the best motives, you may forget events and blessings that are worthy of testimony.

Granted, you probably won't forget the miracles or the more unusual divine encounters, but what about the others? As the years pass, if you lack the opportunity to share them verbally with family or others, you will find these events no longer on the tip of your tongue. They begin to fade.

Sometimes my own stories slide so deep into the recesses of my mind that I recall them only when someone brings up a subject that triggers my memory. But we can't depend on random conversations to activate our testimonies.

A Joshua Project is the only way we can be sure that our memories and our testimonies will endure; therefore, start your list as soon as possible. You will find out why this is such a necessity in the next chapter.

CHAPTER 6

Memory Is a Perpetual Struggle: How Are Your Temporal Lobes Doing?

They shall abundantly utter the memory of thy great goodness.

—Ps. 145:7 KJV

I strode with confidence down the dark passageway, heading to the entryway of my memory. I focused on the event I had come here to recall and tried to open the door. The hinges groaned, rusty with age. I reached out to access that memory and had almost grasped it when the door slammed shut. The memory slid back into my mind's cavernous recesses.

I was trying to recall specifics about something special God had done for me years ago. While I could remember the actual blessing and where I was living at the time, I drew a blank when trying to remember the surrounding details that precipitated it. What happened? Why couldn't I call up the particulars of such an outstanding spiritual event?

It had to be behind that door. But according to the "retrieval failure" theory of memory, my brain had chosen to be selective in what it retained. In this instance, it only remembered the overall impression of what happened instead of the circumstances that led up to it. This selectiveness often occurs when God's concluding act so overwhelms us that the particulars seem inconsequential. As a result, those details fail to establish a strong enough memory pattern to be stored in the brain for retrieval.

Although we can understand why remembering details can be difficult, those details are important to include in one's faith story. Describing the details of life situations so familiar to many of us can convince others that God is mindful of their predicaments, too.

The Importance of Awareness

I often hear people say, "Oh, I don't need to write it down. I'll never forget every single detail of what God did for me in 2001." Unfortunately, I know they are wrong because I know a little about the biology of memory.

When you become aware of the brain's selective memory mechanisms, you will understand how important it is to record accounts of your blessings as soon as possible. Otherwise, important details that should accompany your testimony might be forgotten; yet, we are confident we can recall all the specifics of each supernatural event God ever bestowed. This is because these events so personally impacted our life. Granted, we may not forget the ones involving dramatic miracles, but what about the others, the ones we have categorized as divine encounters?

These less dramatic kinds of blessings can fade into our nebulous past for a variety of reasons, particularly if we fail to share them. If we don't repeat a story often, the brain sets its "fade and decay" device into motion. Sometimes it is only when someone brings up a subject years later that the memory will be activated. Those kinds of memories are described as "cue-dependent," events that cannot be recalled unless certain word-retrieval cues are presented to revive them.

Memory-killing Brain Devices

According to researchers, our recollection of a memory will be influenced by processes that are pieced together like a collage in our brain—devices that affect encoding, storage, and retrieval. The brain draws from this collage of mechanisms, each one having its own unique predilections as to how—or whether—a memory should be stored, what parts should be saved, and how it can be recalled—if at all.

A few of our recall-hindering devices are listed below. This chapter will not delve into all the research and theories related to these processes, but having a simple overview can help you understand why, years later, it can be so difficult to remember.

- **Decay and fade.** Chemicals change our brain when we fail to rehearse an event over a long period of time. Our memory of that event can fade like an old Polaroid print.

- **Distorted (or false) memory.** Existing knowledge and other memories interfere with the formation of a new memory, causing recollection of an event to be mistaken or entirely false.

- **Interference.** Information formatted similarly to a particular memory gets in the way of accurately recalling an event.

- **Retrieval failure.** Neuron-encoding failures and a lack of retrieval cues can make it impossible to retrieve a specific memory.

- **Cue dependence.** Sometimes our memories get so closely tied to subjects, word cues, or other memories, we can retrieve facts about an event only when we are triggered by those associations.

Short-term Memory

Unless you have the excuse of being over sixty and can joke about it, no one wants to admit that their memories are unreliable. But they are. We are definitely "forgetters." This unfortunate phenomenon plagues all of humanity. We know a particular memory is in our head, put there only a short time ago, but we can't retrieve it. Daily experience bears witness to this process.

> Pastor on Monday: "Honey, remind me to pick up the new Sunday school manuals on Friday."
>
> Wife: "Okay."
>
> Pastor on Friday: "Honey, what was I was supposed to do today?"
>
> Wife: "I can't remember. Give me a minute and maybe it'll come to me."

We all experience these types of short-term memory losses. Failing to remember where we placed our keys or our glasses are common and frustrating experiences. We expect such lapses, but we are more upset when we find ourselves losing track of long-time memories that we know are special to us.

Long-term Memory

How does it work? A shocking element is involved in how our brain chooses to handle long-term memories. You may find it disappointing and unfair, but scientists have discovered that long-term memories are not created equal in the brain's memory bank.

Memories are not "saved" in their exact original state, like you would save a document in a computer folder, so you cannot expect to retrieve your recollections with perfect clarity. Each time we access a memory, they are slightly transformed, influenced by one or more of the brain devices introduced above.

Instead of the memory of an event remaining unchanged, psychology expert Kenda Cherry explains, "memories are transformed every single time they are accessed . . . [they are] surprisingly fragile and susceptible to change, misinformation, and interference."[1]

In other words, we could affect our memory if we hear bits of information similar to an already-stored event. When those tiny scraps of information are filed in our brain, they may slide into our memory of the earlier event and become part of it.

"No way! I can remember every jot and tittle. Nothing changes when I recall them."

Everyone likes to believe their memories are photo-perfect accurate. Turns out those memories may be closer to Photoshopped images. Cherry explains how long-term memory works scientifically and what happens in the time lapses between recalls.

> Neurons first encode memories in the cortex and hippocampus. Each time a memory is recalled, it is then *re-encoded* by a similar, but *not* identical, set of neurons. Accessing memories often helps make them stronger, yet the research has found that this *re-encoding* can have an impact on how the information is remembered. Subtle details may change, and certain aspects of the memory may be strengthened, weakened, or even lost altogether depending [on] which neurons are activated.[2]

In other words, the complex mechanistic system inside our brain affects our memories. We have no control over this. These neurons are capricious, with their back-and-forth coding and recoding exchanges, and we are victims of their interplay. In other words, our recall of a memory, especially the details, can be sabotaged.

This also applies to the storing of our memories of godly events. They may have been so dramatic that we will insist a decade later that our memories are still fresh and accurate down to every particular with nothing added or taken away. But that's just not necessarily true. While the overall description of a big event may be the same, the smaller details might change, especially if much time has elapsed since your last recall. Then, when we access that memory and activate those neurons, we may be completely unaware that a detail was left out or slightly changed. The scientific process calls the shots.

How can we ever trust our memories then? There is only one way.

The Solution

Kenda Cherry confirms that "writing down your memory of an important event immediately after it happens is one strategy that might help minimize the effects" of our memory-altering brain processes.[3]

When we record memories soon after an event occurs, with as much detail as possible, we ward off the danger that our faith stories will be transformed ever so little. Fortunately, I journaled about the majority of the testimonies I present in Section 2 of this book, writing down details of those events shortly after they occurred.

When relating an experience recalled at a much later time, it can end up like the proverbial fish story, with the size of the fish growing inch by inch in every telling. This happened to me, and impressed upon me the danger of not writing down details of an event right away.

In 1972, my husband and I went deep-sea fishing on a charter boat off the coast of Eureka, California. You can imagine how proud I was when I caught an eleven-pound silver salmon on my line. It fought hard, and none of the men on the boat, including my husband, believed I could possibly land the fish. They wanted to pull it in for me. No way! I persevered.

Years later, someone mentioned the subject of deep-sea fishing. It triggered my cue-dependent device, and I proudly told the story about the "whopper" I landed. But my fish gained weight in that telling, growing to 12 pounds, while my hands stretched just a bit farther when indicating its length. (I used to think this only occurred in cartoons.)

When I purposely recollected in my mind's eye the scene on the pier, the conversation at the scales, and the register of the needle, I realized that I had added a whole pound to the fish tale, and I made sure I got it right in the next telling. If I had continued to hyperbolize, experts say I would have activated my distorted memory device, implanting this false information so solidly into the original memory that I would have eventually believed my exaggerations were true.

So, how do you let yourself off the hook if you catch yourself telling a fish story or if someone calls you on it? You can't say jokingly, as did comedian Flip Wilson's character, Geraldine: "The devil made me do it." Instead, you can blame the real culprit and tell everyone, "My re-encoding neurons made me do it."

Joshua Understood the Phenomenon of Forgetting

The human race is prone to forgetting and prone to faulty recall when they do remember an event. Old Testament history is filled with examples of Israel failing to remember God and what he did for them. Sometimes, it was because they became occupied with other gods, or proud in their own self-sufficiency. God saw only one solution. His people needed memory aids—well-marked tangible ones.

This is why Joshua was told to memorialize God's miraculous feats not only by keeping a handwritten record and verbalizing the record, but also by building physical objects to commemorate the places where God performed a significant event and recall the occurrence. This was usually a monument of stones (Josh. 4:3–8). Other leaders, including Moses, Isaiah, and Jeremiah, also created physical memorials (Exod. 17:14, 1 Sam. 7:12, Isa. 30:8, and Jer. 36:28).

These visual objects were more effective at creating long-term memories than words alone. Images are indelibly etched directly into our long-time memory; whereas, words we hear proceed mainly into our short-term memory only, where we are capable of storing only several bits of information.

Whenever Israel saw these monuments, they acted as strong reminders of God, his faithfulness in providing for them, his protection in past battles, and their continued need for him. (This is why *The Joshua Project* includes instructions for creating physical memorials to place in the home as visual aids to coincide with your verbalized and written faith stories.)

Generations later, Israelite parents, grandparents, and great-grandparents still pointed to the memorials and recited the historical events, having heard them from the previous generation. Reinforcement came through leaders who periodically rehearsed their history from the handwritten record. Repetition is essential to learning, and God's objective for these memorials and the handwritten records proved effective.

David also understood God's goal when he wrote:

> I will make Your name to be remembered in all generations; Therefore, the people shall praise You forever and ever. (Ps. 45:17 NKJV)

Our Wake-up Call

Yes, we are "forgetters," and we may not always recollect an event accurately even when we think we do. Unfortunately, if we keep our testimonies bottled up in our memory banks without telling or writing them, our faith stories may decay and fade or be clouded with interferences.

A Joshua Project is the only solution to making sure our memories remain sharp during our lifetimes—and for the generations to come.

The next chapter provides the specific, step-by-step instructions for doing just that.

CHAPTER 7

Stage 2: Creating your Joshua Project

I will make Your name to be remembered in all generations;
Therefore, the people shall praise you forever and ever.

—Ps. 45:17 NKJV

We are ready to plunge into the most exciting part of *The Joshua Project*, creating both the Digest version and the Expanded version of your faith stories. They will encourage your family by showing them the great things God has done in your life. They can also inspire questions from friends and acquaintances who may have never heard your stories, and be surprised and encouraged to learn the various ways God intervenes in lives. Your witness will confirm that God is still actively engaged in blessing his children.

Creating your Joshua Project does not require special eloquence, fabulous writing abilities, or amazing artistic skills. What matters is that you create a detailed record of your story and testimony, glorify God, testify to his greatness and goodness, and memorialize his blessings. Often, the simplest expression of words, even if they are not grammatically correct, can touch the heart of readers.

In chapter 8, I provide the instructions for creating physical objects for your memorable memorials so they correlate to the specific testimonies in your Digest and Expanded accounts. To help, I present examples in that chapter from my own Joshua Project.

The Three Forms of Your Joshua Project

Your Joshua Project is designed to be *polymorphic*—which means it's capable of assuming different forms while retaining its inherent identity. By way of summary, the three forms are:

- **A Digest version.** Described previously, this list will be one or two sentences summarizing miracles or divine interventions that have occurred in your life. Hang this list in a conspicuous place in your home so it can generate questions from family and friends. Their questions will give you the opportunity to verbally share the full details of your testimony stories or invite them to read your full account.

- **An Expanded version.** After creating your Digest version, next comes the written version with full details of each event. You can write by hand or use a typewriter or computer. Remember, you are not writing for a prestigious magazine or specialized audience but for your children, grandchildren, and descendants. Just write your stories like you are telling friends about what happened, or sharing your testimony at church. (Appendices I and II offer specific suggestions for publicly sharing your testimony.) Make sure to include details about what led up to the event, describe your reaction, and how you recognized God's hand. After you have created a full account of God's interventions in your life, place your pages in a special three-ring notebook. Or, you can have the book professionally printed and/or bound.

- **Memorials.** You will create one or more physical memorials to place around your home (covered in chapter 8). These objects, visual aids, will serve as a physical testimony to one or more of the events in your written Expanded accounts. They will also inspire questions and encourage gratitude and remembrance of God's blessings in your life.

Let's dive in, starting with the Digest version first.

Your Digest Version

Create a list of all the miracles and divine interventions God has blessed you with in your life. Describe each item on the list in two or three sentences and prepare it so you can hang it in a conspicuous spot in your house. Leave space at the bottom to add items in the future.

The reason you want to create this abbreviated list is because full accounts of each event would obviously take up too much space on your wall. My list, which includes thirty-four events (so far), is printed on four legal-length (8.5x14) pages taped one below each other so as to appear as one continuous document. You can also use 8.5x11 standard size pages and, if you have a large wall space, you can print it out on "landscape" orientation instead of "portrait," which will make the width of the pages 11" (or 14") instead of 8.5. I had less space on my wall, so it is in portrait mode. (see Figure 1 further below).

Pay attention to the following four components as you create this list: (1) format, (2) title and introduction explaining the list, (3) content and conclusion, and (4) decorative embellishments. The decorative embellishments are optional, but they do lend a pleasing look to your list.

Format

Experiment with types of paper, writing materials, fonts, and type sizes for this list. Use paper (white is best) that will make the list visible on the wall but not obscure the contents.

If you are printing your list from a computer program, use an attractive font and experiment with the size. You want it to be big enough to be read easily but small enough to fit on the wall space you have selected. I used Calibri fourteen point, in boldface. If my list had been shorter, I would have increased the font size to sixteen or eighteen points for easier reading. I also taped the printed pages to a large piece of cut-to-size lightweight poster board to make it sturdier.

Your Digest Joshua List will be more attractive if it has a border. If you are creating the list in Microsoft Word, you can add a border at the top, sides, and bottom in color or black. Or you can manually use a ruler and a dark magic marker to draw a border around the printed list (other decorative options are further covered under "Decorative Embellishments.")

Title and Introduction

Place a title at the top of your list. I titled mine "My Joshua List" and included a subtitle and a Scripture, as shown below.

My Joshua List
Commemorating God's Faithful Interventions in my Life

I will give thanks to the Lord with my whole heart;
I will recount all of your wonderful deeds!
(Ps. 9:1–2)

Immediately after your title, create an introduction that explains the contents of your list and your purpose in making it.

Here is my introduction. It is rather lengthy, but yours doesn't have to be:

> Joshua, in his farewell speech prior to his death (Josh. 12; 24) continually had to remind the Israelites of all the specific incidents where God intervened for them—specifically where he gave them victory in battles and enabled them to possess the land he promised. God told Joshua to not only make a physical memorial of twelve stones at the river Jordan, but also write the events down in a book. Why? In this way, Israel and succeeding generations would never forget what God did for them, and determine to always trust and serve him.

> Based on that, I decided to compile my own "Joshua List"—all the moments in my life where God interceded to show his love, faithfulness, grace, love and protection, so that I, too, would never forget. But more than that, I want this list to serve as a testimony to you, my children and grandchildren, of what God is capable of doing, and to know that whatever he did for me, he can do for you. My list below is long, which necessitated it being abbreviated, but the full-length particulars can be found in a special book I have prepared. Its location is mentioned at the end of the list, and is free for the reading. Just ask.

Content and Conclusion

After your title and introduction comes the list itself. You can choose to highlight each item as a numbered or bulleted list or start each as a separate paragraph—whatever works best for you and your list. Set each item apart in your own way.

You might choose to identify the events either by how old you were at the time or by the year it occurred (below, I've included both ways as examples). The two events can be viewed in their Expanded version in Section 2 of this book.

By generating my list on the computer, I was able to accent the beginning phrase of each item in red to immediately draw observers' eyes to that item (although the picture further below appears only in black and white). Or, you could also do as I have done here and simply emphasize them by using boldface type.

Age 4: Saved from drowning in ocean on a deserted beach by a mysterious man who disappeared afterwards.

1957: God spares my life during the birth of my third child, and includes a special message to me.

After completing my list, I added a conclusion and challenged my children and grandchildren to create their own list, as shown next.

To Family and Descendants

The full details of all the above events can be found in a special book entitled, *"My Joshua List: The full account of God's faithful interventions in my life."* It is located at *(describe book and location)*.

My Challenge to You: Compile a similar list of your own life's testimonies about God. They will:

- serve as a reminder to you of all God has done
- instill a stronger awareness of your gratitude to God
- show you that in all life's situations God is faithful, able, and trustworthy
- keep you determined to trust and serve God
- reassure you in knowing that if he did all that in your past, he will do the same in your future
- act as a testimony to your family and descendants

On the following page is my abbreviated list. Due to its length the whole list is not shown.

MY JOSHUA LIST

I will give thanks to the Lord with my whole heart; I will recount all of your wonderful deeds!

(Ps. 9:1-2)

Joshua, prior to his death and also in his farewell speech before he died (*chaps 12 & 24*) kept reminding the tribes of Israel over and over again of all the specific incidents where God was with them—specifically where he gave them victory in the wars they had to wage against their enemies so they could possess the land God promised to them. Joshua's words were recorded. Why? So Israel would *never* forget what God did for them, hoping it would lead them to determine to always trust, obey and serve God. Joshua's list was to act as a reminder for not only the tribes at that time, but for future generations.

I decided to compile my own "Joshua list"—all the moments in my life where God intervened to show his grace, love and protection, so that I, too, would never forget. I am also hoping it will serve as a testimony to my children and grandchildren of the loving faithfulness of God.

4 yrs old: Saved from drowning in ocean by a mysterious man who immediately disappeared afterwards.

7 yrs old: Warned of impending danger by the voice of the Holy Spirit speaking literal words to me, telling me what to do.

11 yrs old: Tuberculosis. God allows me to survive prior years of undetected TB. Scar tissue was discovered in 1943. Reacquired when 23, God healed "overnight."

23 yrs old: Vision of early death of my future husband. Prior to my marriage, God showed me that the Lord would call my future husband (Robert), to heaven early.

1957: God spares my life during the delivery of Debra. As I was going upward to heaven I was given the message that it had been seen ahead of time that I would die during this delivery but God would intervene and not allow it.

28 yrs old: God forewarns me re impending death of my husband. Lord confirms to me via dreams. Also gives Robert a special dream, telling him he will be taken by his 30th birthday.

29 yrs old: Robert dies, freeing me for God to prepare me to leave Mormonism (Feb. 1961, 1 mo. before his birthday), leaving the Lord free to begin opening my eyes to the fallacies of Mormonism and eventually lead me out.

1961 Vision confirming the reality of life after death: At Robert's funeral, God opens my eyes to the reality of life after death. During eulogy, off to one side the air parted like a curtain and I saw Robert dressed in white, seated on a chair with two men in white either side of him, and he was watching his funeral.

1960s on: God begins his work in me:

➢ Supernatural witness that Jesus is the Christ. During a Christmas program at ward, during reading of a scripture.

➢ God turns me on to the Bible and I fall in love with Jesus.

➢ Jesus delivers me from 3, literal demon attacks (my "gold band" experience)

➢ Jesus takes me to heaven to stand before his throne where I experience God's overwhelming love, learn that there is no condemnation for those in Christ Jesus, and have my false Mormon concept of God changed.

➢ God blesses me with discernment when Satan comes to me disguised as Robert.

➢ God blesses me with precognitive dreams (*seeing things ahead of time*), evidently preparatory to the gifts of Prophecy,

FIGURE 1. My abbreviated Digest list hanging on my wall.

Decorative Embellishments

This element is optional, but adding decorations to your list can make it attractive and more likely to catch the eye of visitors to your home, besides your children and grandchildren. And it can be a lot of fun—especially if you are crafty or artistic. If you handwrite your list, you can use colored markers, calligraphy pens, watercolors, etc.

If you have the skills, you can hand-decorate corners and margins, or add scroll-like designs or images such as a small figure of Jesus. If you don't trust your own artistic skills, you can add these kinds of design elements to a computer file by obtaining the images from your word-processing program or importing (copy and pasting) them from internet sites.

To find images online, type "images" then specify what you are looking for in the Google search bar. For example, you can look for "scroll design images," "heart scroll images," "images of Jesus," or images that will illustrate specific stories on your list. Select one or more images you like and save them to your computer so that you can add them into your Digest list document. If you don't know how to save images into your document, go to Google or YouTube and look for instructions based on the computer program you are using.

Or you can skip the computer and use scissors and paste to add images to your list. Cut out images and designs from magazines, religious greeting cards, or personal photographs. Glue the images to your list wherever appropriate. I didn't decorate my list because it was long and I had to utilize all the space.

Your Expanded Account

Your Digest list serves to immediately spread your testimony by encouraging friends and family to talk to you about the items as soon as they notice it. The next step, creating a full Expanded account, ensures that your stories will survive your demise, giving future generations access to your remarkable witness of God's love and power.

There are four short steps involved in creating this timeless treasure: (1) write; (2) compile; (3) create a cover; and (4) leave legacy instructions.

Write

Create your Expanded account from the items on your Digest list. You can handwrite each story, or create the document on your computer. Provide a full account of each event on the list.

Be careful to glorify God and try not to unknowingly exalt yourself. Do not exaggerate or make up details. At the same time, make these accounts interesting for readers by describing details of what led up to the event, where you were, what happened, how you felt, how you prayed over your problem, and how the occurrence has affected you in the time since it occurred. Make your accounts read like first-person stories.

Compile

Choose how you want to store your Expanded accounts. The simplest method is in a three-ring notebook. If you've written your accounts on your computer, print them out and then use a three-hole punch to prepare them for the notebook.

At some point, you may choose to have the contents commercially copied and bound. You can do this at a local printing company, or at businesses like FedEx Office. There is also the option of using print-on-demand services like Lulu, Lightning Source, or Amazon's Kindle Direct Publishing, which would allow you to order bound copies for different family members. If you want to add more stories of God's interventions in your life, you can start Volume Two.

Consider your age when deciding whether to keep your accounts in loose-leaf binders, or binding them into a more permanent form. If you are older and concerned with having your book immediately available to pass down to your family, think about getting it bound right away. If you are younger, keep your faith stories in a three-ring notebook so you can easily add new ones.

Create a Cover

Design a cover for your collection of how God intervened in your life. Also create a title, and be certain to add your name and what readers can expect when they open the printed book or notebook. Here is what I chose to display on the cover of my book:

My Joshua List
The full account of God's miraculous interventions in my life
by
Janis Hutchinson
To be handed down to my posterity

If you are sticking with a three-ring binder, print or handwrite the title on a large label and place it on the outside of the notebook. You might put a label on the spine of the notebook as well. You want to make sure this notebook isn't mistakenly tossed out.

If you are having your book commercially bound, have the title, subtitle, and author's name printed on the front cover. If you decide to use Kindle Direct Publishing or other print-on-demand options on Amazon (mentioned above), consider using some type of picture on your cover along with the title. If you are not savvy about how to do this, you can obtain book cover designs at websites such as coverssellbooks.com/give-it-a-try/ and FiveMinuteCovers.com. Or, you can hire someone to design a cover specifically for this Expanded version.

Further options are CDs (voice recordings), DVDs (video).

Leave Legacy Instructions

Now that your Expanded version has been written and compiled, you want to make sure your family knows what to do with it in the future. Add a note in the front or back of your full account detailing how you want this book to be distributed when you die.

Go one step further and designate in your last will and testament who should receive these written accounts and how they should ensure the book is passed on to future generations. This kind of specific bequest does not normally go within the text of a will but is usually included on a loose, separate page placed at the end, titled "Personal Property." This is where you list other personal items, such as who receives your jewelry, music box, and other treasured objects.

Now, we move on to the next chapter on how to create physical memorials.

CHAPTER 8
Stage 3: Creating Your Memorials

In the future your children will ask, "What do these stones mean?"
Then you can tell them.

—Josh. 4:21–24

Joshua understood the purpose for memorials when God commanded him to collect twelve stones from the River Jordan. The stones were used to create a monument not only to remind the present-day Israelites of a miraculous event, but also to provoke questioning centuries down the line in descendants:

> Then Joshua said to the Israelites, "In the future your children will ask, 'What do these stones mean?' Then you can tell them, 'This is where the Israelites crossed the Jordan on dry ground.' For the Lord your God dried up the river right before your eyes, and he kept it dry until you were all across, just as he did at the Red Sea when he dried it up until we had all crossed over. He did this so all the nations of the earth might know that the Lord's hand is powerful, and so you might fear the Lord your God forever." (Josh. 4:21–24)

This will also be your purpose in creating physical memorials. They will correlate with specific testimonies on your Digest list and Expanded accounts. The aim is to create something visually interesting—like Joshua's pile of stones— to provoke curiosity and questions from children and grandchildren, especially younger ones who may not read yet. Guests in your home may also inquire about your memorials, giving you the opportunity to tell them in detail.

But what kind of memorials work in today's world? Certainly, a pile of stones wouldn't be very effective; yet, the memorial must relate in some way to the event you want to remember.

A greater understanding of memorials in general can help as you consider creating your own. We have already examined several examples of memorials built by Joshua and others in the Old Testament, and we also know they were designed to trigger memories of God's remarkable events. A look at the creation of modern-day memorials, the physical elements they incorporate, and what information they intend to relay, can help us to understand how to create our own objects that will be useful to observers.

Modern-day Memorials

Today's national memorials and monuments, like those in the Bible, also commemorate memorable occasions. They are designed to help people to never forget an event. This is why societies worldwide go to great lengths to erect historic art objects, war memorials, plaques, museums, statues, even colossal archways. All are created to educate future generations about important moments from the past. Here are a few such memorials in our contemporary world:

- Arch of Triumph in Paris honors those who fought and died in the French Revolutionary and Napoleonic wars. It includes the Tomb of the Unknown Soldier from World War I and an eternal flame burning in memory of the unidentified dead.
- Gettysburg, Pennsylvania, contains 1,328 monuments and markers to memorialize the 1863 battle in the U.S. Civil War.
- Mount Rushmore, South Dakota, is home to exquisitely sculpted granite faces of four celebrated U.S. presidents.
- The Statue of Liberty in New York Harbor represents the core freedoms of the United States.
- The Lincoln Memorial in Washington, D.C., honors Abraham Lincoln for saving the Union.
- The 9/11 Memorial and Museum in New York City commemorates those who died in the terrorist attack on the World Trade Center.
- Oklahoma City National Memorial honors the 1995 victims, survivors, and rescuers of that terrorist bombing.

Public memorials like these must obviously be in a "form" that occupies space as a visual centerpiece of the remembrance. They also need to make their purpose known by a dedicatory statement called a "herald," which also needs to be incorporated into your physical memorials.

A Herald

A memorial's herald is a statement explaining its purpose. It can also be called a "dedication." Here are three examples of heralds:

- **The Oklahoma City National Memorial.** "We come here to remember those who were killed, those who survived and those changed forever. May all who leave here know the impact of violence. May this memorial offer comfort, strength, peace, hope and serenity."

- **The Lincoln Memorial.** "In this temple as in the hearts of the people for whom he saved the Union the memory of Abraham Lincoln is enshrined forever."

- **The U.S. Holocaust Memorial Museum, Washington, D.C.** "Only guard yourself and guard your soul carefully, lest you forget the things your eyes saw, and lest these things depart your heart all the days of your life, and you shall make them known to your children, and to your children's children." (Deut. 4:9)

People all over the world purposely visit these visual centerpieces to honor and pay tribute to battles, tragic events, and individual heroes. Generation after generation experience moving emotions as they observe these memorial objects, read their dedicatory heralds, and learn about triumphs and tragedies.

Making Your Memorial

Placed in the home as a visual centerpiece, the physical creation of your memorials should include a herald or dedicatory statement. Like the previous mentioned memorials, it is meant to touch the heart and spirit. Concentrate on memorials to help you remember your most special moments, and also ones you know will bless others when you share them.

Let your creative talents flow when you set out to create these. You can have more than one commemorative object, but don't feel you have to create a memorial for every single testimony you have included in your Expanded accounts. Keep the following three elements in mind as you build your memorials: (1) location, (2) materials, and (3) the subject.

Location

Memorials don't have to be large. They can be any size and can be placed on a small table easel, hung on a wall, or included on mantles or shelves. I believe it is best to place them in the front room or family room where they will be seen by more people. Or you can place one on a dresser in the guest bedroom. Choose what best fits your memorial and your house; also, where it will attract the most attention.

Materials

You can create your memorial from materials you have lying around the house, stored in the garage, supplies you buy in a craft shop, or items you find at thrift stores. You can use a vase, a picture frame, a figurine—even a coffee pot. Of course, you can also create a memorial from scratch if you have the skills. You can paint a picture, or craft a dish containing elements reminiscent of the event. Use or create anything you feel represents the theme of the testimony you want to portray (examples further below).

Another easy way to create a memorial is to display a picture that represents one of your stories and put in a picture frame. You can use paintings, prints, or personal photographs. You could embroider or cross-stitch a depiction of the event, frame it and hang it on the wall in the room where your grandchildren frequently play. These framed objects will catch the attention of your children, grandchildren, and other guests as they move from room to room within your home, piquing curiosity and inviting questions. You may choose to put a small sign at the top or bottom of the picture frame that says, "Ask me about this."

Figure 2 below shows how I used an L-shaped, metal bookend as the basic holder for my memorials. It has a vertical upright part with a tray-like projection on the bottom. The upright part is nine inches tall, but you can find smaller ones that are only five inches. On the tray, I can place any object I want to use in my memorial. (I will refer to the bookend shown in other examples throughout this chapter.)

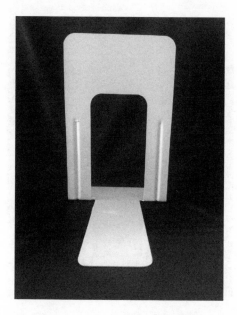

FIGURE 2. Bookend showing upright part and tray-like projection

The memorial shown in Figure 3 on the following page, commemorates a situation where I thought my life would be taken, but Jesus placed a gold band of protection around me. He also opened my spiritual eyes so I could see it (the expanded version is in Section 2 of this book, chapter 16, "God's Gold Band of Protection").

To illustrate this event, I cut out a picture of Jesus and taped it to the upright part of the bookend. To represent God's gold band of protection, I placed a shiny, gold bracelet on the bottom, tray-like projection. For the herald, or dedication statement, I printed at the top, "In memory when God saved my life from the enemy." Below that, I placed these words from 2 Thess. 3:3 (NIV): *"The Lord is faithful, and He will strengthen and protect you from the evil one."* Under that, I placed a typed statement: "Ask me about this!"

Figure 3. Memorial using picture of Jesus and shiny gold bracelet

Next, copying from my notebook of Expanded accounts, I inserted the full story into an envelope and taped it to the back of the upright part of the holder. I positioned the envelope's flap to face outward, so the story could be easily withdrawn and read. To make sure the envelope was clearly visible, I used one that was long enough to extend a little on each side of the memorial, making it visible when viewing the object from the front. At the far, right end of the envelope, to indicate it could be freely read, I put "Read the story in this envelope."

Another of my memorials is the story found in this book's chapter 14, "Power in the Name of Jesus," where God miraculously brought down the temperature in my infant (see Figure 4). On the front extension, I placed a bronzed shoe with a thermometer. At the top is "Ask me about this!" Under that is "Calling on Jesus NAME immediately healed my baby!" Below that is Jer. 10:6: *Lord, there is no one like you! For you are great, and your "NAME" is full of power.*

FIGURE 4. Baby shoe with thermometer

I'm usually home to explain the story to anyone who asks, but the printed story is there at all times if someone would rather read my account than talk to me about it (they may do both). Even if they already know about this event from a previous telling, they may enjoy reading the account again.

Subject

You may choose different types of memorial objects to match your story or event. I've included some ideas here to get you started. Your object can either be placed in some kind of holder, similar to my bookend, or it can be a stand-alone object. I plan to use a mayonnaise jar to create a memorial for one of my faith stories. Sound crazy? See the story in Section 2 titled, "My Mayonnaise Angel." Let your imagination flow. Here are more ideas:

Angels. If you have experienced an angel, either in human or heavenly form, display a statue of an angel. You can make your own or buy one. Many different kinds can be found in thrift stores. Create a dedicatory herald statement to be displayed with your angel that explains your encounter and include a scripture.

Finances. If God provided you with an unexpected financial gift in a desperate time of need, you could use a piggy bank for your memorial object. Write

"Ask me about this!" at the top of a lightweight poster board or piece of strong paper and then attach it to or behind the pig.

Along with the pig, display a herald, such as, "God miraculously supplied my need!" You can also include an applicable Scripture such as Philippians 4:19 (KJV): "My God shall supply all your need[s] according to his riches in glory by Christ Jesus" or 2 Cor. 9:8: "God will generously provide all you need." Tape an envelope containing the full account somewhere on or near the pig, as I described for Figure 3.

Healings. If you were supernaturally healed, you could cut out a picture of a person in a hospital bed and tape it to the upright portion of your holder or bookend. Or display a miniature bed and figure like those used in doll houses, and place them on the front, tray-like projection. Write a herald like, "In memory of the time when God miraculously healed me of a serious ailment." Below that, paraphrase Jer. 30:17: "You restore my body to health and heal all my wounds."

Prayers. Perhaps you heard an audible voice during prayer, or God answered your prayer through an unexpected person or event. Find a small statue of a person kneeling, or with raised arms to God—anything to represent prayer. "Praying hands" are easy to find. Create your herald, display an appropriate Scripture, and include a written account of the event.

Personal memorial objects. This type of memorial is created more for your sake rather than for others. Create one or more to act as a special "reminder" when your faith wanes or you become discouraged.

Instead of including a sign that says, "Ask me about this" on your L-shaped bookend or whatever you choose, use one that says, "(your name), read this when your faith is low." You could display a small statue of a sad person or a sad clown (they're easier to find), or tape an emoticon of a sad or happy face (Figures 5 and 6) to your memorial. You could also place a rock to remind you that Jesus is your Rock. Include a Scripture such as, "For God hath not given us the spirit of fear; but of power, and of love, and of a sound mind" (2 Tim. 1:7 KJV), or "Great is thy faithfulness, Lord unto me" (Deut. 7:9).

Tape an envelope to the back of this memorial that includes meaningful stories of a few incidents from the past that show God was with you. Or include a short sermon written by you or someone else with uplifting and scriptural words. Or, write directly to yourself: "(your name), how can you doubt him? He loves you and has always been there for you. Remember when (describe the event), and remember when (describe another), and remember (another)?"

Figure 5. A sad face

Figure 6. A happy face

After Your Demise

The effort you make to testify to God's love in your life, both in writing (Digest list and Expanded accounts), including creating memorial objects, will prove effective even after your demise. When children and grandchildren read your witness to God's reality, or hear you tell them the story, or touch your memorial objects, their faith will be strengthened, reassuring them that God will do the same for them.

At your passing, your children and grandchildren will likely divide your memorial objects between them as permanent keepsakes. You could even ask family members which ones they prefer and list the recipients for each one with your "Personal Property" bequests in the back of your will.

Summary

Chapters 1 through 8 have helped you gain an understanding of the following:

- the biblical commands given to Joshua and other leaders to make written records and memorials of God's activities;

- the need for testimonies of God in today's secular age;

- the brain's tenuous grasp on long-term memories;

- how to create both an abbreviated Digest list and a full Expanded account of your faith stories to invoke questions from children, grandchildren, and friends;

- how to leave your Expanded accounts of your stories as a legacy; and

- how to create memorial objects as visual aids that testify to your faith stories.

Before you begin writing your Expanded version of faith stories, read the next section of testimonies first. Not only will they serve as examples of how to write your own and how to select confirming scriptures, they will also inspire you with real-life accounts of God's love.

SECTION TWO
INTRODUCTION

Examples of Testimonies of God's Love for Your Joshua Project

I have taken your testimonies as a heritage forever,
For they are the joy of my heart.
—Ps. 119:111 AMP

The main thrust of this book has focused on additional ways to present your faith stories based on Joshua's three-fold model.

This next section presents examples of the faith stories showing God's love and faithfulness that I used in my own Joshua Project with my children and grandchildren. The intent is not only to show you how to write them, but to also demonstrate how to select confirming scriptures to validate the experience.

When you write your stories, please remember, they don't have to be exactly like mine. Many have told me my encounters with God are more dramatic than the norm. I can't help that. They happened, and I'm sharing them. However, your stories don't have to be dramatic to prove that God reached down and touched your life.

Initially, I intended to include only a few as examples, then decided to provide more for two reasons.

First, I was confident that besides using them as examples of how to write them, they would serve to inspire and strengthen your faith.

The second reason is Christian friends have shared with me their concern that they are no longer hearing God's supernatural acts in people's lives at church, and are hungry for them. Hopefully, these stories will fill that void.

My own accounts appear first. Then, a few testimonies from my daughter and son-in-law, Debra and Tony Estes, and my grandson, Isaac Fazio.

I should mention that I also have an additional faith story, "Escape from the Cult," that continues to capture attention from Christian radio and TV shows but is not included in this section. This is due to its length. It relates my experience with Mormon Fundamentalists who held me prisoner for nine months in a small room because I refused to renounce the Christian Jesus. I describe my nearly dying, and how God spoke to me and enabled my escape. This story can be viewed on my blog: wwwjanishutchinson.blogspot.com (no dot after the www).

I hope the following accounts that testify to God's presence and grace in our lives bless you!

CHAPTER 9
Tar Beach

*Are not all angels ministering spirits sent to serve those
who will inherit salvation?*
—Heb. 1:14 NIV

Some . . . have entertained angels without realizing it.
—Heb. 13:2

My favorite outing as a young child, born and raised in Southern California, was when my mother took me to Long Beach, a few miles from our home. There were plenty of long sections along the coastline with the typical breakers that drew crowds. But she did not take me to that kind of beach. I was four years old, and she wanted a safer place for me.

Instead, we went to Tar Beach, an isolated, deserted stretch where my mother and I could have the sand and water all to ourselves. We could look up and down the beach for miles either way and see no one else. This was because it wasn't a popular beach. Not only due to the water having no fun breakers but also because it was loaded with tar, no doubt having drifted from ships in nearby San Pedro Harbor. As soon as we returned home from Tar Beach, I would be placed in the laundry sink where gasoline was used to wash the tar off my legs and arms.

The water wasn't deep there, so my mother thought she could safely sit on a blanket on the beach and read a book while I played in the water. Even as a small four-year-old, I could wade fifty or more feet away from the shore and still only be in knee-deep water.

One unique feature of this beach fascinated me. Here and there were small round hills of exposed sand protruding above the water's surface like miniature islands. They only measured a few yards across, but my great fun was climbing up on each one, then stepping off the other side to wade to the next.

But one day, I stepped off into an unexpected deep drop-off and sank in over my head. Instinctively holding my breath, I became aware of someone grabbing hold of my hair, pulling me up out of the water and back onto the small island. I had no idea who had done this. I just sat on the little hill of sand in shock, staring down at the water I just came out of. That's all I remember of the traumatic incident. My mother had to tell me the rest of the story—and she told it for years thereafter.

She was sitting on the beach reading her book, when she glanced up to check on me and saw a man standing on the small island pulling me out of the water. Where did he come from? Obviously, something serious had happened. How did he know? Who was he?

She leaped to her feet and splashed madly through the water. Reaching the island, she immediately scooped me up in her arms. After making sure I was all right, she turned to thank the man.

"But he wasn't there," she said. "I looked all around. I scanned up and down the long stretch of deserted beach both ways as far as the eye could see, and absolutely no one was in sight. It was impossible. He totally disappeared."

She believed it was an angel in human form.

I do, too.

This was the first miraculous event that occurred in my life—or at least the first I can remember.

Children were always special to Jesus because he knew God had a special place in his heart for them:

> Beware that you don't look down on any of these little ones. For
> I tell you that in heaven their angels are always in the presence
> of my Heavenly Father. (Matt. 18:10)

One of his angels came through for me that day!

> *When you pass through the waters, I will be with you . . . they*
> *shall not overflow you."*
> (Isa. 43:1–3)

CHAPTER 10
Warnings of Impending Danger

You sent your good Spirit to instruct them . . .

—Neh. 9:20

The Holy Spirit is called the "Helper" in the Bible (John 14:26), and he performs his role of instructing in a variety of ways based on the situation.

Occasionally, that role is to warn of danger, sometimes producing an audible voice so distinct you think someone else is in the room speaking to you. I was seven years old the first time this happened to me. However, at that time I knew nothing about Jesus or any Holy Spirit.

My parents were separated. My mother had endured my father's physical abuse a long time in an effort to keep the family together, but when he threatened to kill me and my baby sister, she moved to a small apartment in San Leandro, California.

For some reason, perhaps a reconciliation attempt, my dad arrived one night and stayed over. Things didn't work out, and now, as an adult, I can imagine emotions must have been stretched to the breaking point. This may account for what nearly happened—what could have happened if not for the Holy Spirit's warning to me of impending danger.

The morning after the night he arrived, my dad sat on the couch reading the newspaper. I was on the floor playing with my toy bow and arrow set. The arrows had suction cups on the end instead of points, and I was shooting them at the front door. The old wooden door had a loose window pane in it, so every time the arrow hit, it rattled the glass and shook the whole structure. It was, admittedly, quite a racket—probably enough to stretch my dad's nerves even thinner. If he lashed out, there was no telling what he might do to me. That's when the Holy Spirit moved.

I heard a voice as clear as anything say to me, "Stop—don't do that anymore." I looked around. Who on earth was talking to me? I knew it wasn't my dad—but he and I were the only ones in the room. Even though I knew he hadn't spoken, I asked him about it anyway, thinking he could tell me whose voice I just heard.

"Did you just tell me to quit?" He looked down at me and snapped, "No, but you better stop it anyway!" I did.

Nothing dangerous happened, but the Holy Spirit would not have bothered to speak to me unless real danger was imminent. Years later, my mother told me more about my father's violent temper and what he was physically capable of doing when enraged. I felt he could have turned on me that morning and hit me hard enough to cause very serious injury to me. The Holy Spirit knew this, too, and made sure it didn't happen.

Other Ways the Holy Spirit Can Warn

The Holy Spirit also uses other methods to alert us to danger. He may use a different signal to relay a message such as: "Keep away from that individual—he means to harm you."

Now, I am jumping ahead in time to my adulthood to include two similar experiences to the above one. But instead of a voice, I'm going to relate a different signal the Holy Spirit has used with me as a warning.

After I became an adult, both during my time as a Mormon and later as a Christian, whenever I was unaware that danger was sneaking up on me, the Holy Spirit would cause my insides to start shaking violently in such a strange way that it made me want to get away from a person or a present situation. I only felt this trembling internally; it was not outwardly visible to others. I have learned to pay attention to this trembling because the first time it happened I didn't fully understand what was taking place.

The following story illustrates that first experience and my reaction, but I will keep the account brief to avoid identifying the individual for the sake of the man's family.

I became a widow at age twenty-nine, with three small children to raise; the youngest child barely eight months old; the other two, four and seven. A "man of the cloth" came to offer his help and see if I needed anything. He was kind and thoughtful, and everyone knew him because it was a small town. But as he stepped inside my house and spoke further, the inner shaking began. It became so unusually strong my legs weakened, and I had to lean back on the edge of a nearby table not knowing why this was happening.

After he left, I assumed it was a warning but couldn't understand what it was about. It made no sense, considering who he was. Only later, when this man's inappropriate attentions gradually became more forcible, which included one night he angrily tried to break down my back door when I wouldn't let him in— did I more fully understand the trembling as the Holy Spirit's warning signal.

Indeed, "God's loving protection is great, and his steadfast love shall never depart from us" (Isa. 54:10; Ps. 136:26).

As the years moved on, I discerned that this alert could also apply when something evil was threatening a family member, not necessarily me. In those situations, it was a warning that immediate prayer was needed! Here is that story.

The Holy Spirit's Warning and Safeguard of My Family

When my grandson Isaac was nine years old, he and his mother lived in Texas. I lived in Washington state. His mother had raised Isaac to know his Bible (at his young age, he knew it better than I did), and our family always felt God had a special calling on his life. Nevertheless, Satan, whose mission is to "steal, kill and destroy," tried his best to stop him, beginning when he was a young boy.

Divorce had left Isaac bereft of a dad, and as those early years went by, he grew angrier. Isaac telephoned his dad once, who told him in no uncertain terms he wanted nothing to do with him. As a result, his bad behavior progressed, not only at school but also with the law.

At that early age, he began taking drugs, alcohol, and turned to witchcraft. He was diagnosed by a psychiatrist as bipolar and put on experimental medi- cines. This only exacerbated his emotional problems. He soon became suicidal and was so difficult to handle, one afternoon, his mother had to take him to the ER. They refused to let her take him back home and sent him to a mental hospital facility. I knew nothing about this.

Thousands of miles away, the Holy Spirit alerted me to this serious problem while I was teaching an evening class on prayer at my church. I knew all of the eight attendees well, so it was a relaxed and comfortable setting.

About halfway into the lesson, I began to experience the inner shaking. Puzzled, I kept on with my lesson, at the same time studying the faces of the class members. There was nothing to fear from any of them.

I went on teaching but considered possible scenarios: Is something going to happen to the building . . . an earthquake; a bomb?" I thought of multiple sce- narios as I went on with my lesson, but none of them resonated with my spirit. Still, the trembling continued. I dealt with it as best I could until class was over.

It was very late when I arrived home, and I remained mystified because nothing significant had happened to validate the warning. But knowing the reliability of the Holy Spirit in such cases, I was tempted to call my daughter in Texas but decided it was too late since, timewise, Texas was two hours ahead of me.

When I called her cell phone the next morning, Debra was at the mental hospital. The first thing she said was, "Oh mom, please pray! Something awful has happened to Isaac!" She then explained.

The evening before, Isaac had tried to commit suicide and he was admitted to the facility. From home, he had managed to secretly confiscate fifty pills in his pocket of one of his bipolar medications—one that slows the heart down. He felt no one loved him and decided he would end it all for sure this time. When left alone in his hospital room, he took all the pills and crashed into a deep coma.

"The doctors say there's not much hope," Deb cried. "They injected a kind of tar into his stomach and have used other strategies, but said it was no use. He's still in the coma. Now, it's touch-and-go whether he comes out of it, let alone survives afterwards if he does. They told me that if he comes out of it, he will probably crash again and be gone for good."

The inner shaking now made sense. It occurred at the same time Isaac took the pills the evening before. The Holy Spirit was indeed on the job.

You can imagine all the prayers that went up for that boy as he hovered near death. His mother and I were praying, and so was my daughter's local community, including Isaac's grammar school principal and teachers. His mother and I leaned heavily on Romans 8:28:

> God causes everything to work together for the good of those
> who love God and are called according to his purpose for them.

We knew God had a purpose for Isaac, and we knew that somewhere down deep Isaac loved God. God's calling was still on his life, although he had allowed Satan to take control.

Three days later (amazingly, on Easter morning), Isaac roused from the coma and didn't re-crash. God kept his promise, as he does for everyone when he said:

> I will never desert you, nor will I ever forsake you, fail or aban-
> don you. (Heb. 13:5b)

Isaac never tried suicide again, although problems continued through his teen years. Then, when he was eighteen, God reached out in a final attempt, determined Satan was not going to pluck Isaac out of his hands. I don't intend to relate the marvelous details of that encounter here because in a later chapter in this book Isaac describes them in his faith story titled, "God Didn't Give Up on Me." But here is the update.

Isaac, now lives as a transformed man of God. He helped pioneer a new Victory Outreach Church in Fort Worth's inner city, heading the youth program and street ministry. Totally on fire for God, he shares his testimony at churches, is working toward his ministerial diploma, and hopes one day to go to Asia as a missionary.

The Holy Spirit never sleeps on the job. God warns his children of impending dangers and alerts the appropriate people, as he did with me, so prayer can immediately be initiated and sustained while God works everything together for their good according to the purpose of his plan for them (Rom. 8:28).

> *His faithful love endures forever, and he gives his good Spirit to instruct us.* (Ps. 136:1b; Neh. 9:20)

CHAPTER 11
Healed Overnight of Tuberculosis

I am the LORD, the God of all the peoples of the world.
Is anything too hard for me?
—Jer. 32:27

Tuberculosis is a serious disease and can be fatal. Today, it is one of the top ten causes of death worldwide. It mainly affects the lungs, but it can also affect other parts of the body, such as lymph nodes, bones, kidneys, brain, spine, etc. Symptoms include cough, weight loss, fatigue, bloody coughs, and more. On my mother's side of the family, there were many cases of TB, and my grandfather died of TB of the throat. I contracted TB when I was in my mid-twenties. But it wasn't my first time.

As a young child growing up in the 1930s, I missed a lot of grammar school. I was sickly, always in bed with chest pains, fatigue, weight loss, and coughs; all of which my mother interpreted as bad colds. Therefore, I always stunk of Vicks VapoRub, endured a lot of hot mustard plasters, and gagged over icky cough medicines (no cherry or grape flavors in those days). My mother dragged me from one doctor after another, but none ever thought to take a chest X-ray.

It wasn't until I was twelve that a doctor finally took one and discovered the scar tissue. He explained to my mother that I had suffered from active pulmonary tuberculosis, but said it had eventually "arrested itself."

The doctor who diagnosed me called me into his office, sat me in a chair, and gave me a lecture, wagging his finger at me for emphasis.

"Young lady, I want you to seriously listen to me. To avoid ever being sick again, always go to bed early . . . don't keep late hours . . . stay away from bars . . . never drink . . . never smoke . . . never carouse . . ." On and on he went. I shall never forget it.

The rest of my childhood and early adult years went fairly well, although I was never robust. Then, in my twenties, I became ill again. Regardless of my Mormon affiliation at the time, God was with me again because Jesus promised, "I will never abandon you" (Heb. 13:5). He seemed to have had his hand on me ever since I was little. And, of course, he knew he would eventually be leading me into the kingdom of his dear Son.

I had a friend during that time who had been a nurse in a TB sanitarium, and when she heard my persistent cough and my description of tasting blood and weight loss, she felt sure I had tuberculosis. I also recognized the symptoms from years ago. But knowing there was no cure (at that time), there was no point for me to travel the ninety miles from our desert home on the Salt Flats in Wendover, Utah, to see a doctor who would tell me what I already knew.

I began losing a pound a day and soon became bedridden. I was so weak I could only manage to sit up for ten minutes a day—if at all. At that point, my mother-in-law stepped in to help take care of my two children.

My alarmed husband made a bed in the back seat of our car and insisted on driving me the ninety miles to the doctor in Tooele. When we arrived, even leaning on my husband, it was all I could do to walk into the doctor's office.

Tuberculosis was the assessment, although no chest X-ray was taken. Rather, the doctor wanted to place a tuberculin skin patch on my chest rather than an X-ray so the cost would be minimal for us. If I had TB, there should be a reaction in two days. He also put a patch on my husband.

Hoping for some new scientific breakthrough that could give me immediate treatment, I felt disappointed there was none, but I was too weak to talk much or inquire about anything. Since the trip itself had been such a feat, I knew I could not physically make a return trip in two days, regardless of the skin patch's outcome.

We arrived back home. My husband, an exceptional man of strong faith who truly loved the Lord, more fully recognized the seriousness of my illness. He called his uncle, explained the situation, and asked him to come over that evening to pray for me.

His uncle came, and then left after he and my husband did their praying. I felt so poorly I couldn't see how their prayers would be effective. I knew what I had, how bad it was, and had accepted in my mind and spirit I was going to die. And strange as this may sound, it didn't bother me. I looked forward to going to heaven because I was so in love with Jesus and wanted to be with him. (I had learned a lot about Jesus in the Methodist church before my mother brought me into the LDS Church when I was fourteen). Having this kind of religious death wish, there was no way I could have anticipated what happened next.

The following morning when I awoke, I suddenly sat up by myself (absolutely a miracle), swung my legs over the side of the bed, and stood. I was astounded. What was going on? How could this be? This was incredible!

I gingerly moved with slow steps out of the bedroom and into the front room all on my own, something I had not managed for days. My husband, who was in the kitchen, saw me and stood, dumbfounded. Then he rushed to where I was and began rejoicing, claiming his and his uncle's prayers made the difference. Indeed, I had to admit it. They had prayed the prayer of faith because Jesus said, *"I tell you, you can pray for anything, and if you believe that you've received it, it will be yours"* (Mk. 11:24). He tore the test patch off his chest, and I did the same with mine.

Now, I can hear some of you Christian readers saying, "How could God answer the prayers of a Mormon?" Even the apostle Peter, in Acts 10:34, was shocked at first when God answered the prayers of Cornelius, a gentile! "Then Peter opened *his* mouth, and said, Of a truth I perceive that God is no respecter of persons."

Well, since God is obviously not a denominational God nor a respecter of persons, despite our LDS affiliation my husband and his uncle had faith to believe, and indeed got what they asked for—and overnight! But then, I think God already knew ahead of time he was going to do this:

> I will answer them before they even call to me. While they are
> still talking about their needs, I will go ahead and answer their
> prayers! (Isa. 65:24)

By the second day, I was able to walk to the front door, then the few yards outside to the front gate. There was no doubt. I was healed! We didn't even bother to return to the doctor.

I have progressively learned that whoever dwells in the shelter of the "Most High" will always rest in the shadow of the Almighty. Nothing is beyond the power of God. Jesus explained to his disciples:

> Humanly speaking, it is impossible. But not with God. Every-
> thing is possible with God. (Mk. 10:27)

The reality of being able to rely on God no matter how overwhelming things look has stayed with me throughout the years. I admit there have been times when circumstances bring my faith low, but it soon shoots back up. There are always ups and downs to the spiritual life.

Nevertheless, every morning I tell the Lord the same as the psalmist did: *I bring my requests to you and wait expectantly* (Ps. 5:3).

He is my God in whom I can always trust, knowing he never fails.

> *Give thanks to the Lord, for He is good! His faithful love endures forever.* (I Chron. 16:34)

CHAPTER 12
Halfway to Heaven, But Not Quite

*For I know the plans I have for you," declares the LORD, "plans to prosper you
and not to harm you, plans to give you hope and a future.*

—Jer. 29:11 NIV

In 1960, I was pregnant with my third child. It was a ninety-mile trip to the
closest hospital, so a week before the baby was due, I moved into a friend's house
in Tooele, a few blocks from the hospital.

The doctor had always joked that all my husband had to do was look at
me and I would get pregnant. But it had been different with this baby. We just
couldn't conceive. We kept praying and praying, literally hammering at the door
of heaven for it to happen.

I believe our persistence influenced God to relent and give us our desire.
But in hindsight, I believe it had been the Lord's will I *not* get pregnant because
he knew my husband would die soon. When I became pregnant, we insisted
that this baby be a boy with red hair and, contrary to the usual blue eyes for
redheads, we wanted brown eyes. We got our wish, red hair, brown eyes, and all.
Although neither of us had red hair, it was in our family tree.

But this story isn't focused on the gift of this baby boy. Rather, it's about what
happened during the delivery that verified the reality of God's watchful care and
concern—and yes, even though I was still in the LDS church. Why? Because
before the foundation of the world God loved me, chose to eventually bring me
into his kingdom, and extended his prevenient grace to me because his attribute
is love (Eph. 1: 3-8, 1 John 4:8). That love would be progressively revealed to me
as the years progressed.

Three days before my son's birth, I began losing my water—lots of it. The
amniotic sac ruptured. Most women can expect to go into labor within twelve
to twenty-four hours after their water breaks; but, strangely, losing all that water
did not start labor contractions. When I did start contractions three days later,
they were heavy-duty. I would have, what the nurse later described, as a "dry
birth." I was rushed to the hospital and immediately into the delivery room.

The loss of so much water caused the labor pains to be practically unbearable—worse than the agonizing pain with my firstborn whose head tore all the cartilage out of my tailbone—far worse.

The baby was coming so fast they didn't have time to give me any anesthesia. (I purposely mention this because I have read about doctors who claim out-of-body experiences are simply the effects of anesthesia).

Lying on the delivery table I knew my body couldn't possibly survive what I was going through, and felt I was indeed going to die. Many women use a hyperbole to describe their labor, saying, "It was so bad, I thought I'd die." But my experience was different. I knew with a kind of knowing I can't explain that I was definitely going to die.

At the moment I knew my body had reached the absolute end of what it could endure and my life was going to end, I started to lose consciousness and felt myself leaving my body and going "up." While I was "up there," a message bore into me. This message did not consist of distinct words that form a complete sentence like I'd experienced in other situations in prayer; rather, I experienced a kind of mental communication of the content of God's message as a whole. It relayed to me that before I was born it had been foreseen that my life would be snuffed out during this particular delivery . . . but it was also preplanned that the Lord's hand would intervene and pull me through. I remember nothing after that.

When I came to, I was still on the delivery table and the nurses were giving me a bath. I heard one of the nurses ask the doctor if they should give me a transfusion. He said no, because I had one earlier during my pregnancy. Then the nurses, seeing I had come to, began joking with me. "Not everyone is special enough to get a bath in the delivery room," they told me. They then explained it was because I was totally covered with blood because I had lost so much.

I was still groggy when they wheeled me into the ward and put me into bed, and too weak to physically lift my eyelids open. But as soon as the medical attendants left, I sensed a crowd of people around my bed hovering over me and talking. I couldn't make out any specific words because they were all talking at once. I do remember, however, that their movement and tone of their voices exhibited excitement (that I pulled through?)

When the nurse came in a few minutes later, I was able to fully open my eyes and asked her who all those people were. She told me no one had been in my room; also, that I was actually the only person in the ward. That left me puzzled.

Soon, my doctor came in. The room, of which I was the only occupant, included three or four empty beds on each side with the typical aisle down the center. Instead of his coming to my bedside to tell me about my baby and inquire how I felt, he walked to the far end of the aisle, sat down on a chair, and just stared at me saying nothing. I thought this unusual.

I asked the doctor who all those people were in my room crowding around my bed, and he didn't respond. I asked him other questions, which I felt were routine by a mother who had just given birth, but he didn't answer any of them. He just sat there, stared at me, and didn't say a word. After what seemed like quite a while, he got up and walked out. Mystified by his silence, I remembered it for years. Had he witnessed something supernatural during the time I was going "up?"

I had to assume God spared my life so I could raise our three children after their father died (which would occur in eight months). Perhaps, there was another reason. Who knows?

This I do know. There is indeed a world beyond this one—and there is a God who watches over us. He has "plans to prosper us, not to harm us, and to give us hope and a future" (Jer. 29:11).

> *Lord, you are my God; I will exalt you and praise your name,*
> *for in perfect faithfulness you have done wonderful things, things*
> *planned long ago.* (Isa. 25:1 NIV)

CHAPTER 13
A Special Testimony Given to Me

But I will send you the Advocate—the Spirit of truth. He will come to you
from the Father and will testify all about me.
—John 15:26

Although I was born and raised in the Methodist church, my single mother joined the Church of Jesus Christ of Latter-day Saints (Mormon) when I was fourteen. She was drawn to it, thinking their excellent youth program would be advantageous for me. By age nineteen, I was thoroughly converted to its theology and became active in all its organizations and programs.

I later married a returned missionary, and we had three children before he died in 1961 of spinal meningitis at the age of twenty-nine. I was also twenty-nine at the time. Shortly before he died God had begun to open my eyes to the truth and error of Mormon theology, starting with the incident I describe below, which led to my eventually leaving the church.

Back in the 1960s, the Bible was read in the ward only at Christmas and Easter—or to pull passages out of context to prove Mormon doctrine. Like the average Mormon, I had no great interest in the Bible, focusing only on the *Book of Mormon, Doctrine and Covenants, Pearl of Great Price,* and writings of church leaders. So, what happened that December morning came as a total shock to me.

When I arrived at Sunday school that morning to attend the ward's Christmas program, I sat on the front row. The bishop surprised me by rushing up with an open Bible. Shoving it into my hands, he said, "One of the readers didn't show up. When I give you the signal, come up to the pulpit and read this passage."

I agreed, and put my finger on the place, only giving the words a skim-glance. Knowing most ward members had difficulty reading King James English, I felt smugly confident. *I'll show everyone how well I can read.* Little did I know my cockiness would soon be knocked out of me. I mention this attitude to emphasize that I was in no kind of spiritual frame of mind to self-produce what happened.

Fifteen minutes into the program the bishop nodded to me, and I headed for the pulpit. To this day, I don't remember what passage I read; but it was Christmas, so the verses obviously had something to do with Jesus' birth and his divinity. Of course, I had known from childhood that Christmas was when we celebrated the birth of the baby Jesus, called him the Son of God, sang hymns about him, and exchanged gifts. Then, a few months later at Easter, we talked about Jesus' death on the cross and his resurrection from the grave. It was tradition, and I just accepted it. After all, how could anyone possibly prove something like that? Beyond that, I gave it no more thought.

At the pulpit, I had read only a couple of verses (quite well, I thought, puffed up in self-admiration) when without warning my voice was physically cut off, leaving me absolutely unable to speak.

At that same moment, I felt a powerful "something" come down from above, which I can describe only as like an electric flood of heavenly power. It started at the top of my head and surged down through my body like nothing I can describe. It flowed into my chest, through my arms, down my torso, legs and feet. As it swept through me a powerful voice pierced the deepest core of my inner being: *"Yes, Jesus is the Christ!"*

Then, the surge ended and my voice returned.

Although stunned and shocked, I managed to finish reading the passage. The congregation probably thought I had paused because I had been stymied by the King James vocabulary. I walked off the stage, took my seat, and then left when Sunday school was over.

Moved by the dynamic event and pondering both its physical and spiritual effect, I realized I was absolutely convinced in a way I had never known before— that Jesus was indeed the Christ, the son of God. His birth, death on the cross, and resurrection now took on a much more amazing and personal meaning to me.

Although puzzled by it at the time, in hindsight I can see there were two reasons for that intervention: (1) God knew I was a dedicated, true-blue, through-and-through Mormon with tunnel vision, and that it would take something dramatic to grab my attention; and (2) he intended to use this encounter to launch my journey out of Mormonism.

God had poured revelation knowledge into me—the kind of testimony only given from heaven—not via flesh and blood or others' confessions of faith; nor by logic, intellect, or blind acceptance of some church's written doctrinal statement. No, it was a Holy-Spirit-given witness. It made me recognize that previously I had only an intellectual belief in Jesus. But what I received that morning left me with something profoundly different.

I questioned, "Why did God think my having this was so important?" The Holy Spirit immediately rushed Matt. 16:13–18 into my mind:

> Jesus asked his disciples, "Who do people say I am?" They answered, "Some say John the Baptist; some, Elijah; some Jeremiah or one of the other prophets." Then he asked, "Who do you say I am?" Peter answered, "Thou art the Christ, the Son of the living God." Jesus was especially pleased, and responded: "Blessed art thou, Simon Barjonah, for flesh and blood has not revealed this to you, but my Father in heaven.

I was familiar with the passage because the church used it as a proof text how members' testimony of the truthfulness of the Mormon Church is given to them by God. But the Spirit opened my eyes to something different.

It wasn't about revelation applying to Mormonism, but that Peter had received a revelation about Jesus' divinity. And he didn't receive it from any human source; it came directly from God in heaven. It also meant that Christ's true church would consist only of called-out believers who receive the same kind of God-given testimony. I knew I had received the same kind as Peter!

Many probably wonder how God could have revealed this truth to me while I was still a Mormon. I believe there are two reasons:

- The first can be called "prevenient grace," a term that originated with John Wesley in the eighteenth century. In today's English, it could be restated as "preceding grace"—divine grace that precedes human decision.

- The second reason is that God knew if he intended to bring me out of false doctrine, he had to provide a springboard from which I could be launched. I needed something that would give me a firm testimony and solid foundation under my feet, a Rock I could stand on that would not crumble or shift when I later suffered through the trauma of requesting my excommunication, having friends turn their backs on me, and being pressured to renounce Jesus while I was held prisoner by Mormon fundamentalists.

What kind of difference did that experience make? A testimony about Jesus always draws one to the Bible with new eyes to understand more about him and his divine mission. That's exactly what happened.

The Holy Spirit lit a fire inside me and I was "turned on" to the Bible. I couldn't leave it alone. I became passionate about it, discovering it in a totally new and exciting way. I fell in love with Jesus Christ, his work, doctrines, principles, love, and power. I made posters of eye-opening Scriptures and hung them all over the house. On the wall at the end of my bed, I posted one of my favorite verses, so it would be the first thing I saw every morning:

> I am crucified with Christ; nevertheless, I live; yet not I, but Christ liveth in me, and the life which I now live in the flesh, I live by the faith of the Son of God who loved me and gave himself for me. (Gal. 2:20 KJV)

The blinders fell from my eyes, and I began to be progressively enlightened. Paul states in Eph. 1:18, *"he showers his kindness on us, along with all wisdom and understanding."* For me, these showers included insightful revelations that allowed me to see, for the first time, many problems with LDS teachings which gradually led me out.

God fulfilled his word in me when he said,

> I will send you the Advocate—the Spirit of truth. He will come to you from the Father and will testify all about me. (John 15:26)

It was the beginning of my journey.

> *I will lead [the] blind . . . down a new path, guiding them along an unfamiliar way. I will brighten the darkness before them and smooth out the road ahead of them. Yes, I will indeed do these things; I will not forsake them.* (Isa. 42:16).

CHAPTER 14
Power in the "Name" of Jesus

You can ask for anything in my name, and I will do it, so that the Son
can bring glory to the Father.
—John 14:13

I was still in the LDS Church in 1960 (one year before my husband died) when a special event happened. It occurred after I had been given the special testimony that Jesus is the Christ during the Christmas service and was turned on to the Bible.

I first need to explain that I did not leave right after receiving that testimony. It couldn't happen until later because I had a husband in poor health. Therefore, God planned the exiting of my church for later, after my husband passed away.

In the meantime, God was progressively teaching me new biblical concepts. In the following account, he opened my eyes to something that totally countered what I had been taught.

I had been trained to believe that only men had the authority to call upon the name of the Lord for healings—specifically only those men holding the Mormon Melchizedek priesthood. Therefore, it was a natural assumption for females to believe they had no access to ask the Lord for anything like a healing. They had to request this of two priesthood-holding men because they usually worked in pairs.

I shall never forget the miracle that refuted that false belief.

My youngest son, Van, was born with diseased tonsils and often ran dangerously high fevers as an infant. The doctor said he was too young to have his tonsils removed so we would have to deal with frequent infections for a few years. Since the closest doctor was in Tooele, ninety miles away, at the very first sign of a fever or any sickness we had to begin the long trek and hope we got there in time.

One night took us by surprise.

Van was only a few months old, still small enough to sleep in a bassinette, which we kept in another room that was warmer. Like all good mothers, I rose during the night to check on the baby and discovered he was burning up. His body was jerking, almost on the verge of a convulsive seizure. I grabbed the thermometer, rolled my son onto his side, and stuck it in his precious little butt. I no longer recall what his temperature was exactly, but it was somewhere approaching 103 or 104, higher than it had ever gone before. There was no time to drive to the doctor. And since it was the middle of the night, there was no time to call the required two Melchizedek-priesthood-holding men. Something had to be done immediately.

I dashed back into the bedroom and woke my husband. "Quick," I said. "Get up! We have to pray for Van—and there's no time to call the priesthood."

He scrambled out of bed and rushed to where our son lay. I should have allowed my husband to be the spokesperson since a man was supposed to do the praying. But for a reason I never understood, perhaps out of desperation, I did the praying myself, anxious to get started. My husband didn't object. Perhaps he was too sleepy, or perhaps God intended this for my sake.

We laid our hands on our baby's jerking body. I had read in the Bible that God had highly exalted Jesus, *"and given him a name which is above every name"* (Phil. 2:9); so, I desperately called upon Jesus' name to bring down the fever and save our little son.

During my praying I kept my eyes open, and noticed the thermometer was still in place. I had forgotten to remove it. As I continued praying, I kept my eyes on the mercury level, fearful it would go higher. Instead, the mercury began dropping before my very eyes. I stopped praying mid-sentence. I didn't think mercury in thermometers ever dropped on their own, recalling how I always had to shake them back down to normal after taking a temperature. Nevertheless, I watched the mercury gradually move all the way down to normal.

Van's little body stopped jerking and relaxed. I stood there in shock. There was indeed power in the *name* of Jesus—even by a woman speaking it!

The next day, we phoned the doctor. He decided to start giving him gamma globulin shots, a product derived from bone marrow and lymph gland cells that boosts immunity against disease. Thereafter, Van ran no more high fevers. He was fine until his surgery, which had to wait until he was eighteen months old.

In Gal. 3:28, Paul said there was "neither male nor female, for you are all one in Christ Jesus." Jesus said, "You can ask for anything in my name, and I will do it." Obviously, that did not mean only the early apostles had that right, or only those claiming to hold a special priesthood. Further, that right was not exclusive to men only. I proved that. Any believer, male or female, can call upon his "name" and expect Jesus to respond; the whole point being, *"that the Father may be glorified in the Son"* (John 14:13–14 ESV).

The Father was indeed glorified that night. He is loving, merciful, and he watches over us like he does the smallest sparrow. And there is definitely power in his name!

> *LORD, there is no one like you! For you are great, and your name*
> *is full of power.* (Jer. 10:6)

CHAPTER 15
Jesus Loves Me, This I Know

Jesus loves me! This I know, for the Bible tells me so;
Little ones to him belong, they are weak but he is strong.
Yes, Jesus loves me!
Yes, Jesus loves me!
Yes, Jesus loves me!
The Bible tells me so.[1]

I enjoyed singing that song as a young child in Methodist Sunday school, and it made me know without a doubt someone named Jesus lived in heaven and loved me.

However, I can't say I understood what love was, having nothing to compare it to. I had been boarded out in various homes for many years until I was thirteen. They took me in, as they did other children, only for the money but held no particular affection for me. But I did know how it felt for someone to like or dislike me. Therefore, the song inferred Jesus *really, really* liked me and was the only one in the world who would never *dislike* me. That was the only way I knew to define love.

But, as I was to learn later, there is a big difference between singing about Jesus' love as a child, reading about his love in the Bible, and then having him reveal that love to you directly—which is what he did. Of all the revelatory blessings God has given me over the years this is the one I remember and replay in my mind—even sixty years later.

It happened, back when God first began his preparations to bring me out of the LDS Church and into his truth. First, as told in chapter 13, he gave me an extraordinary testimony at Christmastime that "Jesus is the Christ," after which the Holy Spirit drew me to the Bible where I fell in love with Jesus' compassionate character. For me, it was the first experience of knowing what love felt like.

Nevertheless, I still had a smattering of Mormon theology in me that included a negative concept of God the Father. I envisioned him as a separate being, a glorified man like Jesus, but with a totally different personality. He was stern, ungracious and, as portrayed in the Old Testament, a whip-cracking task-master who demanded "off with your head" for any mistakes.

I'm sure my fear of God was influenced by the LDS Church's impossible mandate of perfection, which I knew I fell short of, and my brief home experience with a strict, earthly father, in whose eyes I could never do anything right. This wrong perception is what led me to focus more on reading the New Testament rather than the Old. I loved Jesus but was afraid of God.

Further, I also had a misunderstanding about forgiveness. My faulty view could be attributed to the unbiblical teaching of LDS Church President Spencer W. Kimball in his book, *The Miracle of Forgiveness*. He stated that individuals could *never* know whether Jesus had forgiven them because there must be "works—many works." This, he said, could take "weeks, it could be years, it could be centuries" before there could be confident assurance of the Lord's forgiveness.[2] This resulted in never being sure if my repentance counted for anything.

In view of all this error, Jesus felt it crucial to correct these misconceptions. He wanted me to learn the truth about God's grace and forgiveness provided through his sacrifice on the cross, and to let me know how much he loved me. He also wanted me to know the true character of God the Father, and how reconciliation with him takes place. Jesus himself stated how crucial this knowledge was:

> And this is the way to have eternal life—to know you, the only true God, and Jesus Christ, the one you sent to earth. (John 17:3)

How did Jesus plan to let me know God's true character and set me straight on so much? Well, here's the story:

One night, I suddenly found myself in heaven in an atmosphere of pure white light, standing before the throne of God. I have no idea if it was a vision, a dream, or if I was "caught up," but I was definitely there. Nothing could have been more real and present.

I looked up the steps leading to the throne and saw Jesus seated in a white robe. Now, one would think I would have been absolutely overjoyed, but fear was my automatic reaction. I felt like Isaiah when he saw the Lord: *Woe is me; I am doomed* (Isa. 6:5).

I lowered my head not daring to look at him, feeling totally guilty, unworthy, and expecting the worst kind of rejection. This response was not some purposeful intention to show a false humility on my part, nor was I thinking about any specific sins. My fearful reaction and awareness of my faulty nature seemed to be an instinctive knowing evoked by just being in Jesus' presence. Not measuring up, I anticipated utter condemnation.

After a few moments, I dared to glance up. Much to my surprise Jesus stood. His face, beautiful, radiant and resplendent, was smiling with a love and acceptance of me that was absolutely beyond description. He slowly descended the steps, and walked toward me arms outstretched; his clear intent to embrace me.

When he wrapped his arms around me, it was a rapturous embrace that enveloped me with an indescribable kind of glorious and exquisite love that no words can possibly relay. My whole being was totally immersed in what emanated from him. I did not need to hear him speak to know he loved me, for it was all relayed through his embrace and the profound acceptance that radiated from his whole being. My feelings of guilt and expectation of rejection immediately evaporated.

But there was also something else . . . I felt it, and it was breathtaking. Not only was I enwrapped in Jesus' personal love, but the entire white, heavenly atmosphere that encircled us was suffused with this same deep kind of love—palpable, like it had a physical presence. I instinctively knew what it was—God the Father's omnipresent Spirit emanating love because it is the very essence of his being. Never had I experienced anything like it!

As a writer, I fall short in my attempt to describe the powerful intensity of God's compassionate nature. No human being could possibly muster up the magnitude of that same kind of heart-love, not even the combined love of thousands of mothers for their children. No tongue can tell it.

Through the years, I continue to marvel. How could someone, especially God, love me that much? But he did! I was *"made right in God's sight,"* as Romans 5:9 says, *"by the blood of Christ who saved us from God's condemnation."* I thought of the hymn, "How marvelous, how wonderful is my Savior's love for me! . . . 'twill be my joy through the ages to sing of his love for me!"

Since that experience, I have never needed to fear about approaching his throne. God's overwhelming love, forgiveness, and acceptance of me, as with all believers, is guaranteed through Jesus. When we understand the truth, and accept him as our Lord and Savior, we can come boldly and confidently into his presence (Eph. 3:12).

When I'm in church, sometimes I look around at the congregation and say to myself . . . "How absolutely wonderful that God loves them with the very same powerful intensity God showed to me. They sing how they love Jesus, knowing he gave his life to redeem them. But I wonder if they really know how much and how strong the intensity of God's love is for them? If only they could experience what I did. They would never be the same!"

I rejoice in my wonderful new relationship with God because I now understand how I was reconciled to him and how *"Our Lord Jesus Christ has made us friends of God"* (Rom. 5:11). Further, I was forgiven on the spot *"to the praise of the glory of his grace, wherein he hath made [me] accepted in the beloved"* (Eph. 1:6 KJV).

My experience, knowing what his love feels like and how it emanates from his very being, is something I have cherished throughout my life. My anticipation is looking forward to heaven and, once again, be enveloped in that same exquisite love.

But that's not the end of this story.

There was another reason God gave this experience to me. In the process of his translating me out of false doctrine and into the kingdom of his dear son (Col. 1:13), he needed to set my theology straight.

So, what was corrected? Three important concepts:

- My belief of a cruel and fearful God was erroneous. His total being is love, not the hard taskmaster I had envisioned for so many years (John 4:24).

- Contrary to LDS teaching, I did not have to perfect myself first with many works and then wait years, even centuries, to wonder if I would ever be forgiven. Jesus, who reflects God's love, immediately loved and accepted me because I now belonged to him. His very countenance and embrace verified Romans 8:1: *"There is now no condemnation for those who belong to Christ Jesus."*

- My Mormon perception of the Godhead, Father, Son, and Holy Spirit, was also corrected. Previously, it had been tritheistic—three separate and distinct Gods, with God as a man of flesh and bone. But I did not see a glorified resurrected man with a white beard who, from a previous world had earned his Godhood (with his many wives), physically sitting on the throne with the resurrected Jesus standing at his side. Rather, God was an omnipresent Spirit, as Jesus himself said in John 4:24, not limited by physical corporeality, breathing out the attribute of his all-embracing love that permeates not only all of heaven, but also resonates through the person of Jesus who is the *sole expression of the glory of God . . . the out-raying of the divine . . . the perfect imprint and very image of [God's] nature* (Heb. 1:3 AMPC).

What a revelatory shock all of it was! The experience affirmed that Jesus died to forgive and reconcile me to the Father, so was qualified to sit on God's throne. Therefore, I am one of those who has been promised to never perish but spend eternity with him and bask in his love forever (John 3:16).

I still enjoy singing "Jesus loves me this I know" . . . but now, it's not only "because the Bible tells me so" but because I understand, having personally experienced it. Even though earlier I had fallen in love with Jesus' character from reading about him in the Bible, my capacity at that level was so limited compared to experiencing the actuality of what the great magnitude of God's all-encompassing and embracing love actually feels like. Knowing that reality, I now better comprehend the Scriptures that try to depict this. Yet, no tongue can really tell it, as portrayed in the hymn, "The Love of God:"

> *The love of God is greater far than tongue or pen can ever tell;*
> *It goes beyond the highest star, and reaches to the lowest hell;*
> *The guilty pair, bowed down with care, God gave His Son to win;*
> *His erring child He reconciled, and pardoned from his sin. (v. 1)*

> *Could we with ink the ocean fill, and were the skies of parchment made,*
> *Were every stalk on earth a quill, and every man a scribe by trade;*
> *To write the love of God above would drain the ocean dry;*
> *Nor could the scroll contain the whole, though stretched from sky to sky. (v. 3)*

> *Oh, love of God, how rich and pure!*
> *How measureless and strong!*
> *It shall forevermore endure—*
> *The saints' and angels' song.*[3]

CHAPTER 16
God's Gold Band of Protection

For we are not fighting against flesh-and-blood enemies, but against evil rulers and authorities of the unseen world, against mighty powers in this dark world, and against evil spirits in the heavenly places.

—Eph. 6:12

But the Lord is faithful, and He will strengthen and protect you from the evil one.

—2 Thess. 3:3 NIV

This is a testimony that involves the reality of the "principalities, powers, and spiritual wickedness in high places," which Jesus demonstrated and Paul warns about in the New Testament, referring to the vast array of evil and malicious spirits who make war against the people of God.

Every culture has recognized the presence of such beings. Today is no different. Billy Graham alerted us to never underestimate Satan's power, or think he isn't real; that we must realize he and his forces will try everything to block God's plan for the lives of Christians. Dr. Russell Moore, Sr. Vice-President at the Southern Baptist Theological Seminary emphasized in 2019, that they will attack us either covertly (stealthily) or overtly (openly). Well, this story verifies these cautionary statements.

This account shows God's power and how far he goes to protect his children against these evil forces. It is also a confirmation of how Jesus *"disarmed the spiritual rulers and authorities . . . by his victory over them on the cross,"* and how Satan and his legions must, therefore, yield to his name—a name which is highly exalted above all names (Col. 2:15).

It happened shortly after I received the special testimony on Christmas morning about Jesus being the Christ and God opening my eyes to the Bible. It was also after I discovered there was power in Jesus' "name" when my baby was dangerously ill. Without the knowledge I gained from both of those experiences, I doubt I would have survived what occurred next. It was something I never could have anticipated.

In a nutshell, the powers of darkness knew what God was doing in my life and did not want me to leave the Mormon Church.

Normally, I had no problem sleeping. But this particular night I was dozing not yet fully asleep, when something dark and evil literally entered my bedroom—not just a single entity, but many. I sensed them the minute they moved through the doorway, detecting not only their presence but also the malevolent, evil-intentioned power they exuded.

Although I intellectually acknowledged God as omnipotent and more powerful than anything in the universe, I was shocked by the forceful intensity of the formidable evil these entities exhibited; it almost seemed to reach a God-like intensity of power. Yet there was nothing godly or good about them. Their essence and life-force energy were venomous—and I did not need to be told they were evil spirits. They didn't just generate fear in me—they generated absolute terror. There's a huge difference. They were worse than the scriptural description of a "roaring lion." Vile and vicious, their obvious intent was to "kill and destroy." I knew I was their focus.

Psychologists may insist I was having the not-uncommon experience of coming out of REM sleep (rapid eye movement) while my brain was still keeping my muscles paralyzed in the sleep state. All I can say is . . . no way.

The spirits moved en masse toward me and came onto my bed. Helpless, I could not move my arms or any part of my body, nor could I speak—not because of the terror I felt, but because their power literally and physically bound me, making me incapable of moving or speaking.

Fortunately, flashing through my mind at that same instant was the Scripture in Luke where Jesus commanded evil spirits to leave; also, the one in John 14 where Jesus gave his apostles power over evil spirits telling them, *"If ye shall ask anything in my name, I shall do it."* I wasn't one of the twelve, but I was desperate. I was also convinced, from the experience with my baby, that Jesus' "name" had power. Would it work?

Unable to speak, all I could do inside my head was formulate the sentence, "In the name of Jesus Christ, I command you to leave."

Much to my surprise and intense relief, the spirits instantly left, but . . . every night, they returned. I lived in constant terror throughout the day, literally trembling physically, dreading bedtime.

After three consistent night visits from the evil spirits, who left when I said the "magic words," as I called them, I knew my life was close to being sucked right out of me. They were going to kill me somehow. Their horrible power during their attacks was diminishing my ability to form complete sentences in my mind. I could no longer construct the full sentence of, "I command you to leave." Either I was getting weaker, or they were getting stronger.

During my next encounter with them, at that frantic moment my mind was sinking so badly I couldn't even recall the full sentence I was supposed to say or think. All I knew is that it was something about Jesus. So, I managed to mentally form the single word, *"Jesus."* It was enough. It worked! They instantly left. I never knew there was that much power in just the single utterance of Jesus' name—enough to overcome the extreme kind of maleficent power those evil spirits expended. Nevertheless, I knew they'd be back.

That next night I knelt by my bed to say my prayers, worn out and weak from the terrifying experiences. I anticipated another encounter but knew I no longer had the strength mentally, spiritually, or physically to fight any more—not even to form the single word "Jesus" in my mind.

The saying, "God helps those who help themselves," went through my mind. I had been taught to believe I had to do ninety-nine percent of the work in order to get God to do his one percent. But as I knelt there, I knew I was totally incapable of even a half percent. I could offer nothing.

So, I prayed, "Lord, if it happens again tonight, I'm just going to have to let them kill me. I have no more strength to fight—not even the strength to say or think your name. If anything's going to be done, it will have to be all up to you." (Perhaps this was the point God wanted me to reach.) I weakly pulled myself up into bed and fell asleep, figuring that night might prove my end.

Sometime during the night, I awoke and once again sensed the awful presence. Scared out of my wits, I kept my eyes closed. But this time, something was different. The spirits were in the room, but they were staying on the far side. Vicious and ferocious, they were fuming, furious, and unfurling extreme rage. To say they were mad is putting it mildly. It is actually beyond words to describe. But what was holding them back from moving toward me?

I dared to open my eyes and raise my head. Much to my astonishment, I saw a brilliant gold band, about six inches wide, horizontally encircling my bed. It made a continuous circle from around the foot of my bed, up both sides, and around the headboard. The evil spirits, who had hopes of killing and destroying me, could not cross over the gold band to get to me. This was why their anger was so fierce and malevolent.

I lay back and relaxed, closed my eyes, and slept in perfect peace the rest of the night knowing God was protecting me with that gold band, and I was safe.

> In peace I will lie down and sleep, for you alone, O LORD, will keep me safe. (Ps. 4:8)

The next day I could do nothing but marvel that Jesus did it all, without any effort on my part. All I had to do was call on his powerful name. No wonder it is "a name above all names!" as Philippians. 2:9–11 states. Moses also knew this:

> Who is like unto thee, O LORD, among the gods? Who is like thee, glorious in holiness, fearful in praises, doing wonders? (Exod. 15:11 KJV)

As a result of that experience, my faith shot up to a level of absolute trust I had never experienced before. It made me so joyful; plus, it gave me a new conception of Jesus. From that moment on, I felt no terror or fear during the day about going to bed at night because I knew that if the spirits came back Jesus would protect me. I could *"lie down unafraid"* (Job 11:19) and could absolutely and undeniably rely on that:

> You will keep in perfect peace all who trust in you, all whose thoughts are fixed on you! (Isa. 26:3)

I also found the gold band itself intriguing. God uses apparatuses? I couldn't get over that. I thought of Job 1:10, where Satan acknowledged God's "hedge of protection" around Job. In that day, hedges of thorn bushes were used to keep wild animals and predators away, so that term was the perfect metaphor for that time period. But perhaps the spiritual "hedge" God put around Job was really a spiritual gold band. The blessing was that he allowed me to see it.

Have other Christians experienced anything like this? I can't be the only one. But I suspect others would probably want to keep it to themselves; it's a pretty extreme story.

Nevertheless, I have no doubt Christians are protected by that same gold band when in dangerous situations, although most are unable to see it. God, in this instance, chose to allow me to see it to strengthen my understanding of his ability, power, and trustworthiness. Satan was defeated, and failed to keep me from leaving the LDS Church.

The Scriptures say that when God brings someone *"out of darkness into his marvelous light,"* they are obliged to tell *"everyone about the amazing things he does"* (I Pet. 2:9 and Ps. 96:3). Further, when he said to *"call on me when you are in trouble, and I will rescue you"* (Ps. 50:15), one cannot neglect the rest of that Scripture which says, *"and you will give me glory."* I hope I have done that.

I have tried to focus this story not on evil spirits but on the power of Jesus who rescues. The whole story is to give glory to him for his trustworthiness.

God is always watching over us, ready to come to our aid, and he has proved many times he is my tower of refuge and strength and a very present help in trouble. From now on I will never fear, no matter what may come.

Psalm 91

Those who live in the shelter of the Most High
will find rest in the shadow of the Almighty.
This I declare about the Lord:
He alone is my refuge, my place of safety;
he is my God, and I trust him.
For he will rescue you from every trap
and protect you from deadly disease.
He will cover you with his feathers.
He will shelter you with his wings.
His faithful promises are your armor and protection.

(Ps. 91:1–4)

CHAPTER 17
Confirmation of Heaven and Life After Death

No eye has seen, no ear has heard, and no mind has imagined
what God has prepared for those who love him.
—I Cor. 2:9

As a young girl, I always had a strong feeling that death was going to come to me early in life. I suffered from poor health throughout my childhood and had received precognitive dreams seeming to verify an early death. Yet, I survived many incidents where I could have died, so this puzzled me. Later in life, however, I came to understand that the dreams and feelings of death pointed to someone else in my family, not me.

Those premonitions of death eventually showed me, as in the following story, how amazing God is, as Psalm 37 states, who *"directs the steps of the godly and delights in every detail of their lives. Though they stumble, they will never fall, for the LORD holds them by the hand."*

First, some background.

I met and fell in love with my future husband, Robert, in California. When we announced our engagement, his parents let me know in no uncertain terms that he was living on borrowed time. They felt I needed to know that Robert's two heart defects and associated health problems were inoperable. Since Robert's birth, the doctor had consistently warned his mother that she should not expect him to live another year, then another year, then another . . . But as Robert grew, his family prayed. As he grew older, he also prayed because he specifically wanted to live long enough to marry and have children.

Knowing Robert's health problems, but seeing that God had extended his life far beyond the doctor's prognosis, I married him. Shortly before our marriage, God gave me another precognitive dream to let me know that the "death" I had been anticipating did not mean me but Robert's, even to the point of showing me the geographic location where it would occur. It was not unusual for me to receive precognitive dreams—seeing things before they happen. But in this instance, I naturally kept this one to myself and never told my husband (I share it further below).

We moved to Wendover, Utah and enjoyed wedded bliss for eight years. We felt God would continue to bless Robert. And God did bless him with life long enough to give him what he prayed for—a wife and children, specifically, two boys and a girl.

One evening, I was sitting at our kitchen table reading when Robert walked in, his hand pressed on the back of his head. He had been having painful headaches for quite a few weeks, which we assumed were caused by sinus problems, never dreaming they marked the onset of spinal meningitis. He stood in the kitchen, looking very serious.

"I have something to tell you, hon . . . I'm going to die soon."

It didn't surprise me.

At this point, I will share the main highlights of the precognitive dream I had rather than all of it because I particularly found it interesting how the Lord used metaphorical images to portray the location where Robert would die, using the geographic setting as the backdrop to the vision. Dreams from the Lord more often come in symbols or metaphors rather than direct messages, and it's up to the recipient to interpret. The ability to accurately interpret develops with time.

The dream showed a lily (representing Robert) struggling to keep moving. Slipping and falling, the lily was unable to maintain its balance on the boulder-strewn terrain, depicting how difficult physical life was for him in real life. Finally, when the lily reached the far end of a long, narrow valley between two rows of rocky mountains, a light pierced the darkness ahead. The glorious figure of Christ appeared. He raised his hand and lightning shot forth, taking the life of the lily that represented Robert.

Therefore, when he walked into the kitchen and made his announcement, I knew the dream was about to come true and it was God's timing. Robert then proceeded to tell me how he knew.

"I received a 'God dream,'" he said. "In it, the Lord told me he was going to call me to heaven. I'm a little confused on the detail of which month," he continued, "but it's either going to be one month before or after my thirtieth birthday." At the time of this conversation, Robert was twenty-nine; his thirtieth birthday would come in five months.

He described the rest of his dream, how he was airborne and shown the majesty of all God's creations. He was taken up into the heavens and transported through the brilliancy of the universe's endless array of dazzling stars and planets, "knowing" he would soon experience all that grandeur and more. His disclosure of his passing didn't seem to upset him; he just accepted it.

I listened to his portrayal of what he had been shown, though he had a difficult time putting it into words. What he described was magnificent. Certainly, I thought,

> No eye has seen, no ear has heard, and no mind has imagined
> what God has prepared for those who love him. (1 Cor. 2:9)

Why did the Lord let me know of Robert's death so many years prior? So that when he was taken, I would know it was definitely God's will. Like the lily stumbling over life's boulder-strewn terrain portrayed in my dream, Robert's health and struggles every day were becoming so difficult, he had reached the point physically where he began voicing the wish that the Lord would take him. It was time.

Therefore, anticipating his departure in five months, we planned for it by living out of our food storage. This way, we avoided spending money at the grocery store, and paid off the few bills we owed so I wouldn't be left with any debts.

A few months later, Robert's mother took him to his doctor in Salt Lake City for a throat culture. She thought his headaches had been going on too long. With his heart condition, the doctor was always concerned about the slightest infection.

Because it took two or three days to get results from the culture, Robert and his mother traveled on to Ogden to stay with his sister and wait for the results. I remained behind in Wendover with our three children, who were eight months old, four, and seven.

One evening during the three days Robert and his mother were gone, I stopped abruptly while ironing Robert's green work uniforms. A message from the Lord came clearly: He will never wear them again. Accompanying it was a "final" feeling, the kind I've received more than once when I've learned ahead of time that others were going to die. I rolled up the uniforms and placed them back into the laundry basket. The very next day, Robert's mother called to tell me he had been rushed to the Ogden hospital with spinal meningitis.

I arranged for a relative to take care of the children, then sped the 159 miles to Ogden.

Robert died one day later, one month before his thirtieth birthday in the midst of Utah's Rocky Mountains, at the far end of a long, narrow valley-corridor known as the Wasatch Range. It was the location I had seen in the dream prior to our marriage.

I didn't grieve to the extreme, since I had been prepared all those years. I felt grateful to have been chosen to be part of God's plan for my husband, so he could have the longevity and the children he prayed so earnestly for.

Knowing what a long physical struggle life had been for him, any sadness at his death was made comparatively light. Further, God, heaven, and life after death were such realities to me that when everyone said, "Robert is dead," it didn't ring true. To me, he was just as alive in heaven as he had been on earth.

But that isn't the end of the story.

At Robert's memorial service, I was sitting on the front row listening to the eulogy, when I looked off to my right. A section of the air suddenly parted like two stage curtains being drawn aside, one to the right, the other to the left. A portal was revealed where I could see into the other world. There, in a very "white" atmosphere, sat Robert on a chair, his legs crossed. He was dressed in white, and nonchalantly watching his service while two men in white stood on either side of him. I assumed they were angels of some kind.

I especially noticed how unmoved Robert was over the proceedings. I suppose I shouldn't have been surprised; after all, didn't the Lord tell the apostle John on the Isle of Patmos that there is no sorrow, crying, or pain in heaven? Death is simply a relocation of the person from one place to another. Therefore, what did Robert have to be sad about? He had simply passed from this world to the next. Life was continuing for him, and he was still alive, just as Jesus said in John 11:25:

> I am the resurrection and the life. Anyone who believes in me
> will live, even after dying.

Although I can't prove it, I gathered from that experience that all those who are called to heaven may have the same privilege of watching their own memorial service. If so, how gracious the Lord is to allow the departed to hear the nice things people say about their life. I am grateful the Lord blessed me to see my husband. It gave me added confirmation of heaven's reality.

While many may not receive the gift of being shown events ahead of time, God still speaks, directs, and blesses all of us in different ways. Sometimes, when a loved one is taken, God may simply direct the Holy Spirit to supply the *"peace of God that passes all understanding"* (Phil. 4:7 KJV). Therefore, no one need experience anxiety over the matter.

God proved Psalm 37, and directed Robert's steps until it was time for him to be taken. He also ordered my steps so that I could be used to fulfill my husband's prayers of living long enough to be married and have children.

Jesus told us that in his Father's house are many mansions. God definitely had a place prepared for Robert. One is also prepared for me, his three children, grandchildren, and the rest of his posterity. God promises this for all those who love him.

Along with Paul, we can praise the Lord because:

> Through the eternity of the eternities, we shall ever be with the Lord." (1 Thess. 4:17 AMPC)

> *The LORD directs the steps of the godly. He delights in every detail of their lives. Though they stumble, they will never fall, for the LORD holds them by the hand.* (Ps. 37:23–24)

CHAPTER 18
God's Love–Surprise

You will seek me and find me when you seek me with all your heart.
—Jer. 29:13 ESV

Now widowed with three small children, there came one cold gray winter evening when God suddenly emerged from his mysterious hiding place to make himself known to me in a more personal way. Even though I had not yet "officially" come out of the LDS church by requesting my records be removed, I was still enjoying the new insights and revelations God was giving to me. But what happened that particular evening was unexpected, and it shocked me to the very core.

After putting the children to bed and stoking the fire, I settled back in my La-Z-Boy and reached for Saint Augustine's *Confessions*, an old book I had picked up earlier at a garage sale. Flipping through the pages, I stopped when a chapter heading caught my eye, "Looking for God in the fields of memory."

Intrigued, I read the whole section of Augustine's analytical search for God. I enjoyed his thought-provoking questions, particularly this one: "How is it that after finding God we recognize him, when we never knew him beforehand?" His answer, however, disturbed me.

According to Augustine, the ability to recognize someone or something can only come from our memories, so that is where God can be found. When we re-examine our memories, no matter how horrendous, we will find God in the midst of our story.

I bristled with indignation. If there was *any* truth to Augustine's claim, then I should be able to ascertain if God had been in my life by simply recalling my life's experiences. I could remember every crucial event that took place in my childhood and I knew for sure that God was definitely not in those moments, albeit he had been showing up on occasions in my adult years. (It was only years later after this incident I'm about to share, that I recalled my mother's story of my childhood experience at Tar Beach, and how the Holy Spirit had warned me about my father when I was seven.)

At this point, all I could think about was my earlier years which had been filled with hurt, ugliness, and my feelings of not being valued–especially from the people I boarded with who put me down all the time. Therefore, I felt I understood God's reluctance in not being there for me—there was certainly nothing likeable or loveable about me.

As I reminisced, I tried to recall any major incident in those early years that made sense. If I could find just one, then maybe I could say God had been there. But there was no rhyme or reason to any of it.

Grabbing a pencil, I began formulating a response to prove Augustine wrong. But the long day suddenly began to take its toll and I leaned back wearily in my chair. Resting with my eyes closed, I experienced something completely unexpected.

All the past events of my life erupted in my brain, the unexplainable setbacks and tragedies with their defeats, failures, and disappointments. It was like watching a movie of my life—including scenes I thought I had buried so deeply I would never have to look upon them again.

I pushed the unwelcome scenes aside, but they kept reappearing, as if pleading for some purposeful explanation; I could not cram them back into the dark recesses of my mind. In fact, I could do nothing but helplessly succumb as all the tangled, chaotic events of my life rushed forward in all their unintelligible disorder. I could find no purpose in these unwelcome and unbidden thoughts— it was like trying to read a story of incoherent sentences and out-of-sequence paragraphs. But they did confirm what I already knew about my early life: God was never there for me.

In that dozy state between sleep and wakefulness, I watched a full rehearsal of the unhappy events of my childhood and teenage years—the good, the bitter, the perplexing and distressing. It was like watching a movie, complete with a soundtrack that was harmonious at times, dissonant and tuneless at others.

I watched myself act out the old, pitiable scenes, one after the other. The entire cast was there—estranged relatives, friends, acquaintances. I re-experienced childhood fears; saw myself boarding in unpleasant homes after my parents divorced; suffered again through surgeries, tuberculosis, chronic health problems, and near-death situations. All of it revealed one indisputable truth: My life was worthless. No one cared, not even God.

Then, still in this dream-like state, I became both player *and* viewer. As actor, I was aware of my interaction with others, but as viewer I was standing far off and observing the whole production. I could see players concealed offstage waiting for their cue to enter. My attention was suddenly drawn to one in particular. Who was that? I didn't recognize this person. I hadn't noticed him while I was the actor. Then, slowly, I realized . . .

It was God!

There he stood in the middle of my horrible story, completely absorbed in the sometime discordant music playing in the background, measuring the tempo, calling the cues, skillfully directing and orchestrating all the scattered pieces of my life.

Under his commanding gestures, the chaotic and fugue-like events of my life whirled together in a spinning maelstrom of soul-awakening harmonies. Rhythms, patterns, order, and disorders—all the counterpoints of my life—moved in all their crescendos and dynamics, collaborating in a strange synthesis of unity and diversity.

I soon noticed, in the midst of all that swelling cacophony, something surprising taking place. All the disordered array of tuneless dissonance began to fuse into a single, euphonious composition. Every event and episode of my life became a musical note, the value of each note depending upon the preceding one and also determining the quality for the next notes to come. The arrangement blended into soul-stirring, cathedral-like chords.

Flowing from one to the other, even the ill-sounding notes mingled and merged with the more melodious ones into a connective continuity. Melding into a dynamic whole, the fragmented events were no longer disconnected incidents but a divine continuum. God was taking up all the jumbled scraps of my chaotic life and arranging them into a definitive pattern—structuring the harmony and melody of me! I watched in amazed delight.

But as with all compositions, the notes of my life's events gradually began to dissolve into silence, leaving only their combined effect to linger in the last reverberating tone. And in the flow of quiet that followed, like the interpretive hush after the concluding strains of a magnificent symphony, the impassioned final note echoed, punctuating the full meaning of my schizophrenic existence, revealing purpose, design, and significance.

I now had to acknowledge a divine structure where I had believed none existed, a stability I had thought missing, a reality I assumed was not there. God had always been there, guiding and watching over me. He did love me after all during those times!

I have no idea how long the experience lasted, but when I opened my eyes my first impulse was to leap to my feet, applaud, and shout, *Bravo!* Not for myself but for God, who had been wielding the baton and orchestrating my life all along!

Moved to tears, I experienced a brokenness that surpasses description. My zero-level image of myself changed, and I saw the *real* me as desirable to God. I saw him as the ever-faithful Lover and myself as the Beloved. He cherished me just as I was, in the midst of all the unfortunate situations, the messiness, fears, and mistakes. In return, I loved him back with a love that was indescribable.

I immediately fell to my knees to express my gratitude—to call upon his name and try in some way to say, "thank you." But as the words formed on my lips, I panicked. They fell short. Those two words did *not* express what I was feeling!

Groaning in frustration, I groped for some way to rephrase it with more meaning. But there were simply no words in my vocabulary to express what I was feeling.

In a final moment of utter helplessness, I cried out: "Lord, how can I say thank you?"

To my surprise, distinct words flooded into my mind—discerned so clearly it was as if God himself stood in the room next to me. The compelling message came powerfully and yet gently, peacefully and reassuring:

"Let your light so shine before men, that they may see your good works, and glorify your Father which is in heaven." (Matt. 5:16 KJV)

I was dumbfounded. That's how I'm supposed to say "thank you?" In joyous relief I responded: "Oh yes . . . I will!"

In the gratifying days and years that have followed, I continue to bask in the wondrous afterglow of that experience—and in the assurance that no matter how many discordant, chaotic, and tuneless scenes lie ahead, God will be there in the sidelines, faithfully guiding and orchestrating the whole wondrous composition of my life.

Augustine was right. It is at the point of deep introspection and the strangeness of remembered experiences that God's presence can be found.

> *Lo, I am with you always [remaining with you perpetually— regardless of circumstance, and on every occasion], even to the end of the age.* (Matt. 28:20 AMP)

CHAPTER 19
Miracle in the Mountains

I will give you back your health and heal your wounds" says the Lord.
—Jer. 30:17

For some reason, God didn't stop me from doing the following. Why?

I was nearly ready to withdraw officially from the LDS church but had always wanted to live Brigham Young's United Order, which is sharing, and having all things in common, like the New Testament saints did in Acts, chapter 4. I believed this was the way God wanted us to live.

Therefore, I joined a Mormon Fundamentalist group, an offshoot of the mainline church, where I could experience that lifestyle. Why didn't God stop me? I learned later, he had two reasons.

First, he knew Fundamentalists possessed historical records and accounts handed down from Joseph Smith and Brigham Young's day that would verify in black and white for me the definite falseness of Joseph Smith as a prophet, his church and temple work—information unavailable anywhere else. This was before the Internet, and those books and documents were not yet available to the public. His second reason was that I would need that factual information for future books I would write.

Once in the group, I read and devoured everything. Soon, I was totally convinced of Mormonism's errors and fully embraced biblical truth. The decision also included the United Order itself after seeing the leader's forceful exercise of unrighteous dominion and suppression of free will.

I began sneaking away to a Christian church, was followed and discovered. The leader demanded I renounce the Christian Jesus. When I refused, he held me prisoner for nine months in a small room, where I nearly died (full story on my blog).

After escaping in 1979, a severe hemorrhage required six blood transfusions, followed by major surgery. I was also left with other serious problems. Crippling pain spasms shot through my neck and back like electric volts. They hit without warning, bringing me to the floor. I also had a completely paralyzed colon and suffered from extreme weakness and fatigue. All in all, I lived in a continual state of illness. But unbeknown to me at the time, God intended to keep his promise in Jer. 30:17 when he said, *"I will give you back your health and heal your wounds."*

However, he wanted to teach me a few things first—especially about himself. So, when I moved to Parowan, Utah, a sleepy community of fewer than 2,000, and attended a small Christian church—my first after leaving Mormonism—this move proved God-inspired because it led to my miracle in the mountains and what God wanted me to learn.

Through the devoted efforts of church members continually praying for my health problems, all my ailments were healed except one—my paralyzed colon. Continually sick and in pain, with the medicine the doctor prescribing proving more debilitating than the condition, I was soon advised that I was facing complete removal of my colon. I panicked. *Not that! I don't want to wear a bag on my side for the rest of my life!* I determined to give prayer more time.

The church's devotion continued. They were still laying hands on me, praying and authoritatively declaring, "You're healed!" But I saw no evidence. I couldn't understand why their prayers didn't seem to be effective for this ailment after they had worked for my other ones. They told me, "You already have your healing. Just keep claiming it or you will lose it." It sounded like the burden of the matter was now falling on me to bring this about.

Desperate to be healed, I decided to exhibit stronger faith. I quit taking my medicine while continuing to pray, pronouncing my declarations of healing, and claiming it.

By the end of that week, I was really sick. I was definitely *not* healed. My prescriptive prayers weren't working—neither were the prayers of others. Was it because I couldn't "muster up" enough faith at the moment they were praying over me? How much did God require? Or was this kind of health problem too much for the Lord to handle? Discouraged, my faith sank lower. I felt depleted physically, mentally, and emotionally.

Then something different happened . . . which led to my mountain miracle testimony.

Every year, the Parowan church conducted an old-fashioned, week-long camp meeting in the nearby mountains of Parowan Canyon. A huge tent was erected, and Christians from all over the United States attended. I had never been to a meeting like this before. The music was great, with lots of exuberant singing and praising the Lord, and I should have been as enthusiastic as everyone else; yet I wasn't. My body, as well as my faith, was drained. I was especially depressed because blood spots had now visibly forced their way through from my colon onto my stomach. Surgery needed to be done soon.

On the second day of the meeting, I was at my lowest ebb. That's when I totally gave up. I felt no hope of God ever coming through. Despite my experience twenty-three years earlier of being healed overnight of tuberculosis, my faith disappeared entirely. I decided he just didn't want to do it.

One of the speakers that day was a minister from Colorado. He started preaching and, like some Christian preachers do, would interrupt his sermon and declare a "Word of Knowledge" to announce that someone in the crowd was being healed of a certain ailment.

"Someone is being healed of nicotine," he shouted.

Fake, I thought. *Out of the hundreds that are here, he knows his statement is bound to apply to someone.*

He continued with his sermon, then stopped and spoke another "word." But this time it wasn't so generic. Rather, he named every single symptom I had, down to the most minute detail. His description was so thorough that my daughter and the pastor's wife immediately rushed over to me.

"You're healed! That's got to be you. How else could he know all that?"

"Healed?" I smirked, and pulled up the bottom of my shirt, tugged the waistband of my slacks down a little and showed them all the blood spots that were breaking through onto my stomach. "Seeing is believing," I said, "and I'll believe it when I see it. It's all in God's lap now. He can do it, or not do it. I'm not trying anymore."

I left camp meeting and drove home discouraged as ever . . . that is, until late that afternoon—when I realized I was healed!

It staggered my imagination. I kept walking around the apartment I shared with my daughter, shaking my head and exclaiming over and over, "Deb, I can't believe it . . . I can't believe it . . . I'm healed!" I kept that up for two to three days. It had to be the biggest miracle in my life up to that point, including my tuberculosis.

What puzzled me later was this question: "How come I was healed during a time when I was not exhibiting any faith at all—not even any power-of-positive-thinking, affirmative declarations, or naming and claiming it? And on the day I was healed, I had demonstrated absolutely nothing in the way of faith—at least what I assumed God expected on my part to prompt a miracle.

I was left with only one conclusion. God moves solely on his own volition, and that one's faithful praying does not always obligate God to move immediately no matter how words are formulated. Neither does it manipulate him into moving before he is ready. While scripture assures us that he hears all prayers, his supernatural acts in response are entirely self-motivated, initiated by his own passionate love for us and his grace . . . but *only* when he decides the time is right.

James 5:16 tells us that the prayers of many "availeth much"—and I still believe in having others pray for us because the many prayers of those in the Parowan Church were effective and I was healed right away of my other ailments. But in some instances, he decides when to move, perhaps when he knows the greatest lesson will be learned by the recipient.

What did God want me to learn from that last healing? He wanted me to know that he didn't want me to exert anything on my part that I could interpret later as *my* controlling or forcing his actions.

Scripture says we are saved and healed by his "grace," not of works lest any man boast—and after all that time and effort I spent claiming and naming, I certainly could not boast that all my repeated affirmations and declarations manipulated or forced him into healing me. It was after I gave up my own efforts, that he did it.

Jer. 1:12 says that he is *"always alert and active, watching over his word and his promises to perform it in our lives."* He was obviously alert and active to see that he performed one particular promise for me: *I will give you back your health and heal your wounds* (Jer. 30:17).

He didn't do it right away, but perfectly timed it when he knew I would better understand his love, grace, and especially his sovereignty.

> *You, O Lord, are a God of compassion and mercy . . . and filled with unfailing love and faithfulness* (Ps. 86:15)

CHAPTER 20
The Fragrance of Angels

Those who take the Bible at full value cannot discount the subject of angels
as speculation or hollow conjecture . . .
If you are a believer, expect powerful angels to accompany you
in your life experiences.

—Billy Graham, Angels: God's Secret Agents, 29 (first ed)
—Billy Graham, Angels Around Us, Daily Devotion

I was baptized in the Parowan, Utah church in 1980 to testify to my profession as a new Christian. I learned much in that little church, but I had never heard of the fragrance of angels. So, when it happened to me, I was full of questions.

"Pastor, how can a floral scent waft in front of my face in a closed-up room with no flowers present?"

"That's the fragrance of angels," he explained. "It's their way of letting you know they are present."

He and his wife, raised in an earlier church culture where Christians weren't hesitant to report such encounters, were familiar with the experience. The general understanding was that angels may sometimes announce their presence with a fragrance to let someone know God is aware of their situation. Many who have experienced this phenomenon are reluctant to report it, but some have, describing a flowery sweet perfume like roses, lavender, or lilies. I experienced a fragrance like a mix of roses and carnations.

I had no doubt angels existed. The Bible contains nearly 300 references to their activities, and God is the same yesterday, today, and forever, so I was sure he still used them in the variety of roles related in the Scriptures.

But I didn't understand why angels were coming to me in this aromatic manner. Was it to let me know that my leaving the LDS Church was right, and they were there to help me get through the aftermath of transitional problems I was still dealing with? Those were indeed difficult days, and many times I was on the verge of giving up, so the following account proved significant.

I attended the Parowan church with my adult daughter, Debra, who had also left the LDS church after God opened her eyes while on a Mormon mission. My first job in the church was teaching the children how to make hand puppets, and fashioned a large puppet stage (like the old Punch and Judy booths) so they could perform simple Bible stories for the congregation. In preparation for the Christmas program, I purchased art supplies to paint elegant backdrops such as scenes including the wise men and shepherds. It was a true labor of love, and I was excited about it. Debra helped me as I created the scenes on my kitchen table.

As I finished painting each scene on poster boards, I carried them into the bedroom and placed them on top of my bed to dry. My bedroom at the time was larger than the normal bedroom, about 13x23 feet. The size is important to my story.

On my second trip into the room with the art work, I detected the angel's fragrance. I knew the aroma was coming from only one spot in the room, extending from the floor straight up as in a column, like a person's single body standing tall. I experimented by walking about the rest of the large room. The fragrance was nowhere else. When I returned to the same spot, it was still there.

I returned to the kitchen and told Debra an angel was in the bedroom. I had told her about my previous encounters like this one, but she had never experienced the fragrance.

"It's in a certain place," I said. "I'm not going to tell you where. Go in there, and walk around the room. If you detect it, point to where it is. If you indicate where I already know it is, that will certainly confirm the reality of the angel's presence."

She walked in, while I stood in the doorway watching. She circled the large room and suddenly pointed to the same spot where I had encountered the fragrance. "Oh, Mom, it's right here!" She was elated—her first time to breathe in the angelic aroma.

"Move around the room again," I said, "and see if you sense it anywhere else." She did.

"No, Mom." She walked back. "It's only in this spot." She pointed again to the exact place, a big grin on her face.

We felt this was a testimony that an angel was overlooking and approving what we were doing in our new Christian church experience. Actually, I believe it was particularly meant for me, yet it also confirmed to Debra that my former accounts of angelic presences were true.

It has been decades later, and angels still make their presence known to me in this way. Sometimes the room will suddenly fill with the fragrance when I am preparing a Bible lesson for a class. One afternoon in particular, I was struggling to figure out which of two themes to focus on in a particular Bible chapter. I went back and forth over my options. Frustrated, I finally decided on one, heaved a big sigh, and said aloud, "Well, they're all good. I sure hope this is the right one." Instantly, the fragrance wafted in front of my face. God, through his angel, wanted to let me know I made the right choice. Heb. 1:14 tells us angels are spirits sent forth to minister those who are heirs of salvation.

I am continually filled with joy that angels still choose to let their presence be known to me with their fragrance. Knowing God cares for me this much—as he does all his children—inspires me to walk in faith, trusting in his watchful care. Billy Graham said, "When we know God personally, through faith in His Son, Jesus Christ, we can have confidence that the angels of God will watch over us and assist us because we belong to him."[1]

> *Believers, look up—take courage. The angels are nearer than you think . . . God has given his angels charge of you, to guard you in your ways.*[2]

CHAPTER 21
Hearing God's Audible Voice

Thou calledst in trouble, and I delivered thee; I answered thee in the secret place of thunder [and] the Lord thundered from heaven, and the most High uttered his voice.

—Ps. 81:7; Sam. 22:14 KJV

After I finished teaching puppetry in the Parowan church, the Holy Spirit dropped a special ministry gift on me. I was used to public speaking, having been trained in the LDS Church in a variety of leadership positions, but this new and different calling of one of the Holy Spirit's gifts caused me to literally shake in my boots.

Although I felt inept in stepping forward and speaking in this new capacity, I did it out of obedience. But fear overwhelmed me every time, keeping me in a perpetual state of stress and anxiety. I knew this was a special God-calling, and not just some other job in the church that I had a choice of accepting or refusing. Nevertheless, I was on the verge of asking the Lord to remove this obligation, so I spent two full days fasting and praying, literally morning to night, telling God I wanted to do his will and asking for support and aid in overcoming my fear.

I didn't expect a vision or anything dramatic. I just hoped that God would dispel my anxieties and somehow make me competent and able. I certainly didn't expect anything like what happened.

After my second day of praying, I awoke one night to see two angelic beings in white standing by my bedside. They laid on hands and prayed for me—or I should say their hands hovered over me because I couldn't feel their touch. I heard no words, yet I knew they were praying about this ministry gift I was on the brink of renouncing. When through, they moved a few feet away, knelt on the floor facing each other, and bowed their heads together in silent prayer.

At that point, for the first time in my life, I heard the mighty and powerful voice of God—not just words internally within my mind or heart, like the Holy Spirit often does—but external to myself.

It began with a forceful and dynamic rolling-type of thunder that at first was distant but gradually grew closer, becoming louder and louder. When God finally spoke, his voice was not only in the thunder but was the thunder.

Though his words were directed to me, the sheer magnitude of his utterance resounded through the entire length, width, depth, and breadth of space and everything in existence—not only our forty-six billion light-years of known universe and two trillion galaxies, but beyond, much wider and far-reaching—as if there were other immeasurable, vast expanses of the universe on a scale far beyond what I could ever conceive. His voice filled every bit of it, and he blessed me to intuitively comprehend this. It was almost as if I were seeing it.

What did he say to me? Albeit only five words, I cherish them so much I have chosen to keep them to myself (sorry to disappoint you). Nevertheless, the awesomeness of his voice (which I noted was strongly male) and the whole encounter was overwhelming. It was something I shall never forget, although my attempt to describe it falls way short.

This type of external hearing experience rarely occurs more than once or twice in a person's lifetime—if it occurs at all. Recipients of such a holy and amazing experience can rarely find words to portray it. Yet no fear is felt at the time because the peace of the Holy Spirit prepares hearts for the encounter.

What happened after that?

The following Sunday at church, it became evident God had miraculously resolved the situation. My anxiety and stress were totally gone, and I had relaxed power to function in what I had been called to do . . . all to the glory of God.

Three truths were confirmed in the way God chose to answer my prayer: (1) the reality of his existence beyond any doubt; (2) the literalness of asking in faith and receiving; and (3) the prayers of the two angelic beings verifying Hebrews 1:14: *"Are they not all ministering spirits, sent forth to minister for them who shall be heirs of salvation?"* Further, my account testifies that God still moves in his children's lives as he did in Bible times.

I searched the Scriptures to find anything comparable to what I experienced. Sure enough, I discovered similar descriptions of God's voice:

- Listen carefully to the thunder of God's voice as it rolls from his mouth." (Job 37:2)

- Moses spoke, and God thundered his reply. (Exod. 19:29)

- I heard a sound from heaven like the roar of mighty ocean waves or the rolling of loud thunder. (Rev. 14:2)

- The sound of his coming was like the roar of rushing waters. (Ezek. 43:2, also, Rev. 1:15)

- Then I heard again what sounded like the shout of a vast crowd or the roar of mighty ocean waves or the crash of loud thunder. (Rev. 19:6)

Other biblical characters likened his near-deafening voice to a trumpet blast.

- The first voice which I heard was as it were of a trumpet talking to me. (Rev. 1:10; 4:1)

- For they heard an awesome trumpet blast and a voice so terrible that they begged God to stop speaking. (Heb. 12:19)

On the internet I found a few other people who were brave enough to admit God had spoken to them in a "thunderous" voice external to themselves. All noted as I did that his voice was strongly male. The accounts did not go into detail, and I suspect it was for these reasons: (1) they found it challenging if not impossible to find appropriate words to describe the experience; (2) are hesitant to mention it because of its supernatural nature; and (3) feel it was a sacred experience, the kind not usually shared with others. Even I was reluctant to include my experience in this book.

Why did God give this experience to me? He knew it was vital. I had barely come out of the LDS Church into Christianity, and he knew I needed all the evidence he could provide so I wouldn't return (not uncommon). My transition from Mormonism to Christianity was admittedly rocky, and I was on the verge of returning many times despite knowing their doctrines were unbiblical.

God kept me grounded in the truths of Christianity through many supernatural experiences that ultimately proved to be for his glory.

The long-range intention of God's grace, in whatever manner he chooses to extend it, is always for his glorification.

> And as God's grace reaches more and more people, there will
> be great thanksgiving, and God will receive more and more
> glory. (2 Cor. 4:15)

In the years that have passed, God has since spoken to me many times through the Bible, or through the Holy Spirit via a mental impression, a message to my heart, or a voice inside my spirit. But I have never had another experience to match the magnitude of that evening. As with David, I can only say, "Praise God, who did not ignore my prayer or withdraw his unfailing love from me" (Ps. 66:20).

> *This is the confidence we have in approaching God: that if we ask anything according to his will, he hears us. And if we know that he hears us—whatever we ask—we know that we have what we asked of him . . . so that the Father may be glorified in the Son* (I John 5:14–15; John 14:13 NIV)

CHAPTER 22
The 1,500-Mile Prayer

The effectual fervent prayer of a righteous man (or woman) availeth much.
—James 5:16 KJV

How many physical miles will God travel to fulfill a prayer request?

The answer came as a complete shock to me. The supernatural story that unfolded to provide that answer proved even more amazing.

The pastor and his wife, in the Parowan, Utah church, were totally committed to helping me undo the mental baggage most ex-Mormons bring with them, but I had countless doctrinal questions. They did their best but couldn't answer many of them to my satisfaction. So, at fifty years old, I decided I needed to go to Bible College.

I began sending for catalogues, gathering facts, studying and comparing colleges. It never dawned on me to go to the Lord and ask him which college I should attend. After all, doesn't God help those who help themselves? What difference would it make to him which one I attended, as long as I acquired the needed education? I had no idea God might have something else in mind.

I received various Bible College catalogs, meticulously studied the curriculums and costs, and narrowed my list to four: International Bible College (IBC) in San Antonio, Christ for the Nations in Dallas, and two others, the names of which I've since forgotten. After more intense study, I selected Christ for the Nations. I became so excited and could hardly wait to tell the Lord where I planned on going!

After work, I raced home and dashed through the front door. Bolting into the bedroom, I slid on my knees to my bedside. Wasting no time, I blurted out, "Guess what, Lord? I'm going to Christ for the Nations!" But before I could get another word out of my mouth, I was interrupted as I heard literal words:

"No . . . San Antonio!"

I sat back on my haunches in shocked puzzlement. After a few seconds, I let out a long breath, "Well, so much for the best-laid plans . . . I guess it's IBC."

I had no idea at the time that God's insistence, to the point of letting me hear actual words, did not mean it was a better college than Christ for the Nations but that he was in the process of answering the prayer of an eighty-eight-year-old woman who was 1,500 miles away in San Antonio. The unfolding of this experience would prove to be one of the greatest examples of God's love in answering and fulfilling the prayers of his children.

So, in 1981, I packed my bags, threw them into my car, and off to San Antonio I went, not knowing why.

The first morning in the chapel, the president of the college greeted the new students. Needless to say, I was the oldest female there, and with my premature white hair I'm sure I looked even older—probably ancient to the rest of the students, most of whom were just out of high school or in their early twenties.

In the course of his lengthy speech, the president mentioned his eighty-eight-year-old mother-in-law, Anna Schrader, who needed caregivers around the clock. She was mentally alert but physically too frail to fix meals and care for herself. He said remuneration would be applied to tuition for anyone interested in working for her. The job required spending the afternoon, evening, and night with her, bathing and dressing her in the morning, fixing her breakfast, and then returning to school for classes, making room for the next shift. The job didn't interest me. I had money saved up for two years of tuition and had paid in advance, so I dismissed the announcement.

My first day of classes fascinated and excited me, and at home I eagerly plowed into homework, burning the midnight oil. Because of my heavy academic load, I thought no more about the words the Lord had spoken to me back in Parowan. I was used to receiving direction from the Lord and decided he must have directed me to IBC because it was simply a better college.

I never expected what happened next.

For three nights in a row, the Lord kept me awake showing me a woman's face. There was absolutely no letup. I tossed and turned. Sleep was impossible. Though I didn't recognize her, I somehow knew this was the president's mother-in-law. Lack of sleep dragged me down during the day, and I realized if I was going to get any rest at night, I had to go to work for her even though I didn't need the money.

I went to the college president's wife (the registrar) and explained what was happening. "If I don't go to work for your mother, I'm never going to get any sleep."

I don't think she really understood what I had been experiencing, but she set up my schedule for the week to alternate with other students' shifts, and then added, "My mother is a very godly woman, and even at her age still has a weekly radio program called Sweet Hour of Prayer. She tapes it from her home and I mail it to the station for her."

So, I went to work for Anna Schrader and the persistent night images quit. I saw no need to mention them, although they still puzzled me as to why. Also, I thought no more about the Lord telling me to go to IBC as studies totally occupied my mind.

One morning, after bathing and dressing "Sister Schrader," as we were told to address her, I knelt at her feet putting on her hose and slippers. She glanced down at me, cocked her head with a knowing look, and asked, "Do you know why you are here?"

"No." I looked up at her, puzzled at her question. "Actually," I began, "I had no financial need to work for you except that—"

She interrupted me, and smiled. "It's because I prayed you here."

Something extraordinary began to resonate, and I recalled the Lord's direction I received in Utah.

This sweet, gentle lady then told me about her prayer to the Lord, which included her displeasure with the young girls the college was sending over.

"They don't understand my needs," she said. "They do a poor job, get out of patience with me, and complain when they have to get up during the night to tend to my needs. They were making my life miserable. Desperate, I decided to make it a matter of prayer.

"I told the Lord, 'Please bring someone closer to my own age to take care of me. Also, I need someone to transcribe my tapes and help in my radio ministry.' You, Janis, are the answer to that prayer."

Finally, all the pieces fit. I told her my full story about hearing the command to go to San Antonio and the persistent night images of her face. She marveled at my story, then lifted her face toward heaven and praised the Lord for answering her prayer to bring someone 1,500 miles away who originally had no intention of attending IBC. It was a marvelous testimony of how far God will go to answer the prayers of his children.

Sister Schrader and I got along famously. We developed a great rapport and very close friendship. I continued working for her for four years and became her codirector, helping tape her radio programs. When time for Christmas vacation came, she made her lament apparent. She didn't want me to leave her. So, I gave up my two weeks plan I had of visiting my mother in Utah, and stayed to work for her.

This gentle soul wanted me there practically all the time, and insisted I be with her when she breathed her last. This came at age ninety-three. And I was definitely there for her.

The verse quoted beneath the title to this story, "The effectual prayer of a righteous person availeth much," was not intended to refer to me, but to that godly woman, Anna Schrader, who trusted her Father in Heaven would supply her need.

Distance is no problem for God.

> *Behold, I am the LORD, the God of all flesh; is there anything too difficult for Me?* (Jer. 32:27 AMP)

CHAPTER 23
A BULLET IN THE CHEST

The Lord is good . . . He cares for those who trust in him.
For he will order his angels to protect you wherever you go.
—Nah.1:7 NIV; Ps. 91:11

In San Antonio, I graduated from IBC with my bachelor's degree and ministerial diploma. As valedictorian of my class, I was able to enroll in the university on a scholarship and earn my master's degree in theology. A classmate introduced me to his church which I began attending, although it was miles away on the opposite side of the city from where I lived. I chose the earliest worship service so the rest of my day could be spent on homework.

This particular Sunday morning I was on the I-410, called the "Loop," driving the inside lane (the one next to the passing lane). This five-lane freeway was usually deserted during those early hours, and I rarely saw another car.

But that morning, there was one sole black car in the right lane next to me, about six or seven car lengths behind me. In the rearview mirror I could tell it was one of those cars sleeked up by teenagers, with a lowered rear end, the back bumper hanging just inches from the road.

Suddenly, the Holy Spirit spoke to me with unusual force: *"You're going to be shot with a bullet in the chest!"*

I panicked. I had received warnings like this before, and I had no doubt it was going to happen. The only one who could possibly shoot me would be the driver in the car behind me. My panic increased as I looked again in my rearview mirror and saw he was pulling closer, the front of his car now even with my right rear bumper.

I had planned to shoot my car off to the right across the five lanes and get off the freeway at the next exit; however, the black car was so close I couldn't pull over without running into it. I would have to wait until it passed. I white-knuckled the steering wheel and held my breath. Was he going to pull out a gun and shoot me as he passed? Fear tensed all the way to my feet.

I watched as his car pulled up on my right, the driver's window open. The driver was a young man in his late twenties, noticeably skinny. To my surprise, he paid no attention to me—didn't even look over at me—and gradually pulled ahead of my car. Nevertheless, still feeling the warning inside me, I gunned the engine, shot my car over to the outer lane, and exited as soon as I could. I then took the backroads to church.

Although puzzled over the incident, I returned home after church and focused on my homework, mostly forgetting about it. That is, until I walked through the front room and happened to glance at the news on TV that evening and saw reporters and policemen surrounding an automobile wreck. I widened my eyes. It was the same sleeked-down black car I had seen on the freeway.

The car door hung open, and the body of the skinny driver was slumped over the steering wheel, one leg draped out of the open car door . . . dead. I immediately recognized him. The narrator said he had been "shot in the chest by a sniper on the freeway." No doubt by the bullet that would have hit me!

Did I feel lucky? Yes and no. I grieved over the young man's life and went through survivor's remorse—feeling guilty for eluding death at someone else's expense.

I thought about this young man, wondering what plans he had for his life, pictured him hanging out with friends, laughing during happy times. I pictured his parents mourning the loss of their son. Could I have done anything to warn him? No. Because I didn't know he would be the one to be shot—I thought he was the one who was going to shoot me.

Further, I could not have stopped the sniper. Sadly, there will always be people like that, intent on causing harm to others. God doesn't choose to step into this fallen world to stop all the Hitlers and terrorists. Earthquakes, tornadoes, floods, and other disasters also strike. Why do some escape while others don't? We don't know why. Life happens—it isn't always fair.

But I am convinced I would have been that victim on the six o'clock news if the Holy Spirit hadn't warned me to pull off the freeway when I did.

God promises in the Bible to watch over and protect his children. I'll never know why I survived and not the young man. Not having the answer but knowing God did warn me, I praise him for watching over and protecting me for reasons known only to him.

> *The LORD will protect you from all evil; He will keep your soul.*
> *The LORD will guard your going out and your coming in from*
> *this time forth and forever.* (Ps. 121:7–8 NASB)

CHAPTER 24
My Mayonnaise Angel

Those who take the Bible at full value cannot discount the subject of angels
as speculation or hollow conjecture . . . angels have not
infrequently assumed visible, human form.
—Billy Graham[1]

The following may sound like the craziest testimony you ever heard. I almost didn't include it until I read a similar one in a book by Dr. Jane Glenchur, *Seven Secrets to Power Praying: How to Access God's Wisdom and Miracles Every Day.*[2] I also heard her share her similar testimony in a TV interview, and I'll include her story after mine.

Both her story and mine confirm that God cares about the little things and that his angels are only too eager to be of service. My story happened after I had graduated from the university in San Antonio and moved to Everett, Washington.

I needed a jar of mayonnaise—and bad.

It had to be a quart size because it needed to last all month. Since I am gluten-intolerant and have to use gluten-free bread for sandwiches (ugh), I need mayonnaise to make them palatable. I'm also very health conscious, so the mayonnaise, besides being gluten-free, also had to have acceptable ingredients.

My fixed income was meager, so I counted the nickels and dimes in my coin purse. I had a dollar and some small change—all I had left until my next check. Could I even find a large jar of mayonnaise for that little? I remembered that most of them were usually two dollars and up.

At the time, I was recuperating from leg surgery due to a torn meniscus and could barely manage walking because of the pain. I knew I couldn't walk around and push a grocery cart, but knew a huge grocery discount store nearby had plenty of electric carts—if I got there early enough in the morning. Sitting in a cart, I could sail down the aisles and rest my painful leg.

I was in luck. The store at that bleary-eyed hour was practically empty of customers, so I settled into a cart, headed for the condiments aisle and parked in front of the mayonnaise shelves. That's when I gasped in dismay.

There were way more shelves of mayonnaise than I had remembered. Towering way above me, the section was seven feet high, eight feet wide, and contained every different brand of mayonnaise you could imagine. I was overwhelmed. How could I find the right kind of mayonnaise with the right kind of ingredients for the right amount of money without spending an hour or more? I couldn't even see the top shelves from my cart. Standing would cause too much pain. At that moment, I felt totally helpless.

In my peripheral vision, I noticed an older man in a knit hat walking rather quickly down the long aisle toward me. He passed behind me, and leaned over barely breaking his stride. Pointing to a specific jar on one of the lower shelves, he said: "That's the *best* one." Without another word, he continued down the aisle.

I took the jar from the shelf and examined it. Gluten free, included the perfect ingredients, and the price matched the little bit of money I had. I was elated. It would have taken me forever to find that specific jar.

I turned to look in the direction the man went, wondering how he could have known exactly what I was looking for. It was an extra-long aisle, typical of super stores, and I didn't think it was possible for him to have exited it in those few short seconds. But he was nowhere in sight.

I put the mayonnaise in my cart, pressed the "go" lever, and headed down the aisle, hoping to find and thank him. Surely, he had to be just around the corner. If not, his knit cap should make it easy for me to identify him, especially since the store was still practically vacant.

I searched up and down every single aisle in the whole store—all twenty-three of them! I also examined all the checkout lanes. The man in the knit cap was nowhere to be found.

I pulled the cart into one of the checkout-stands, paid for the mayonnaise (with two cents left over), and drove home marveling at my prized purchase. Still, I felt badly I didn't have the chance to thank the man. I continued to puzzle over the whole scenario. No regular customer in the store could have passed me that quickly in the long aisle, known exactly what I was looking for, and pointed it out. Could he have been an angel? But in the mayonnaise aisle?

I recalled a passage from Billy Graham: "Angels are real. They are not the product of our imagination, but were made by God Himself. If you are a believer, expect powerful angels to accompany you in your life experiences."[3]

I could believe that God would send an angel to save a four-year-old from drowning, like he did for me, but would he be concerned about my dilemma over something as trivial as a jar of mayonnaise? I had to conclude that he would.

Later, as if God wanted to provide me with a divine confirmation, I happened to turn on a Christian TV interview and heard Dr. Jane Glenchur describe a similar incident.

Her young daughter had spilled juice on the carpet, leaving a terrible orange stain. She didn't discover it until days later. In desperation, she prayed, "Lord, help me find something to get rid of this stain so that she [her daughter] won't feel bad about the spill (and so I won't be upset!)."

Dr. Glenchur dashed off to the store, only to encounter numerous stain removers lining the lowest shelf, each claiming to be the best. She was grateful she had arrived at the store at an early hour so there would be no one to see her down on her hands and knees, scooting along the floor and asking God which stain remover was the best. Even as she asked, she wondered if God really cared about something so insignificant:

> With a smidgen of faith and a mountain of self-consciousness,
> I placed my hand on top of a can of cleaner, closed my eyes
> and asked God, *Is this the right one?* I waited a few seconds. No
> answer. What was I expecting, thunder from heaven? I moved
> on to the next. Nothing.

As she placed her hand on the next can, she heard a voice behind her. "That is the best stain remover." She saw two white-haired women passing in the aisle. They repeated their words a second time, then a third as they passed by. She bought the product, and it worked marvelously on the stain.

According to Dr. Glenchur, that incident revolutionized her shopping experiences. She concluded that if God cared about a carpet stain to send angels, she could utilize his wisdom for other purchases. She told about other God-directed store purchases in answer to prayer, all of it bearing out the truth in Philippians 4:6–7:

> Do not be anxious about anything, but in everything by prayer
> and supplication with thanksgiving let your requests be made
> known to God. (ESV)

How do we know we can always let God know our requests and that he will do something about them?

This is the confidence that we have before him: that whenever we ask anything according to his will, he hears us. And if we know that he hears us in regard to whatever we ask, then we know that we have the requests that we have asked from him. (John 5:14–15)

My story and Dr. Glenchur's story demonstrate how God cares, no matter how small the issue. She prayed, and God answered. I hadn't even prayed about the mayonnaise, but God still cared anyway.

You can be sure that God will take care of everything you need, his generosity exceeding even yours in the glory that pours from Jesus. Our God and Father abounds in glory that just pours out into eternity. (Phil. 4:19–20 MSG)

CHAPTER 25
Healed Instantly of Glaucoma

Are not all angels ministering spirits sent to serve those who will inherit salvation?
—Heb. 1:14 NIV

This is a rather amazing story that involves a miraculous healing in a medical problem, and two angels. The Scriptures testify that:

> He is the faithful God who keeps his covenant for a thousand generations and lavishes his unfailing love on those who love him and obey his commands. (Deut. 7:9)

In the following situation, he really came through!

After extensive tests, the eye doctor had given me the dreaded glaucoma diagnosis and prognosis. He even showed me the picture of the hemorrhages behind my eyes. He sent me to an ophthalmologist, a glaucoma specialist in a nearby town who verified my condition. I was to keep seeing both doctors but only needed to return to the ophthalmologist every six months.

Knowing the condition was irreversible, I matter-of-factly accepted it, although I worried about how it would affect my writing ability at the computer. At that time, I had written three nonfiction books and a novel, and was also writing articles for my blog and communicating via email as a mentor in the Mormon Mentoring program for the Institute of Religious Research, a Christian counter-cult ministry.

My daughter, Debra, is a true prayer warrior. She lives in Texas, and whenever I'm ailing she is quick to stand in for me at her church for prayer. I had no idea she planned to initiate prayer for me that Sunday. Nor was I thinking about my glaucoma as I sat in my Sunday school class that morning.

But that's when it happened. I felt a spiritual *whoosh* go through me. I recognized it from past experiences with the Lord but had no idea what it related to this time. Puzzled, I glanced at the clock on the wall and noted the time. I then refocused on listening to the teacher's lesson.

When I arrived home, my daughter telephoned.

Mom, this morning at church when the pastor asked if anyone needed prayer, I jumped out of my seat and ran forward to stand in for you. He prayed for your glaucoma, and just as he finished praying, he added, "Oh, there are two angels that are rushing right now to heal your mother."

I shared with her about feeling the spiritual *whoosh* and checking the clock. We confirmed the time difference between our two states (two hours) and realized the pastor's prayer occurred within a few minutes of the moment I felt the spiritual power go through me—obviously, the action of the two angels. I was excited that my next meeting with my eye doctor was scheduled soon so I could find out if the healing was total.

The doctor routinely ran me through the normal time-consuming tests. While he went to get the print-outs of the tests, I waited in his office. When he brought in the reports, he was shaking his head. "I don't understand it. All your tests are normal."

He sat down at the computer and pulled up the previous pictures of my eyes, showing me the hemorrhages and past test results. He then glanced back at the new report and said, "It makes no sense why your tests are normal."

Knowing glaucoma never reverses itself, I decided to push him into some kind of explanation, wondering what he could possibly say.

"Doctor, do you think my glaucoma has simply gone away . . . on its own?"

He paused, and then hesitantly said, "Well . . . I guess . . . so." He sent his findings to the ophthalmologist who, on my next visit with him, confirmed I no longer needed to see him.

I was thrilled and couldn't keep from praising God, especially since I had accepted my condition as final and hadn't even prayed about it. But God said,

I will answer them before they even call to me. While they are still talking about their needs, I will go ahead and answer their prayers. (Isa. 65:24)

He honored my daughter's and her pastor's prayer, who was aware that two angels were on the way.

Are not all angels ministering spirits sent to serve those who will inherit salvation? (Heb. 1:14)

True to the Bible, *"The prayer of a righteous person availeth much"* (KJV), and *"the prayer offered in faith will make the sick person well [and] the Lord will raise them up"* (James 5:15 NIV).

God has been blessing his children, answering their prayers. and healing them since the beginning of time, and employs angels to carry out his will. God's scriptural promises can be trusted, and his words are enduring. I'm proof of that.

You don't always have to "feel" something as I did to know when God or his angels are doing something special. There have been times when he has done something for me and I felt nothing supernatural or any indication that something was about to happen.

Just accept on faith that God keeps his promises and will do what's needed in his own timing, and never doubt he responds to prayer requests because, *"No word from God will ever fail* (Luke 1:37 NIV).

I can definitely testify with Ps. 36:5 (NIV), *"Your love, Lord, reaches to the heavens, your faithfulness to the skies,"* and the words in the following hymn:

> *Great is thy faithfulness, O God my Father;*
> *There is no shadow of turning with Thee,*
> *Thou changest not, Thy compassions they fail not,*
> *As thou hast been, Thou forever wilt be."* [1]

CHAPTER 26
God Knows My Name!

I will praise the Lord, for he has shown me the wonders of his unfailing love.
He kept me safe.

—Ps. 31:21

When I first became a widow at age twenty-nine with three small children, eight months old, four and seven, I wondered at that time if God knew the physical and emotional hardships I was going through. Though I loved him and prayed to him, was he only present in a general kind of universal way, or did he know me personally—I mean *really personally?* Like, did he know my name? The answer came on a night I'll never forget.

Normally, I slept like a log. Why? Because I was plumb worn out. In the small, desert town I lived in, both coal and wood were used to heat homes. Lugging heavy coal buckets from the huge pile in my back yard into the house was back-breaking, let alone chopping wood. Then, periodically came the grunt job under the house of taking the huge, dirty furnace ducts apart to clean out the built-up creosote and soot; also, having to climb on the top of the house in the bitter cold of winter to fix roof leaks, taking in ironing to financially survive; not to mention, wearing myself to a frazzle with the children. I was in a state of exhaustion all the time.

That night, nearing gale force, the winter wind's bitter gusts howled around the house. I placed an extra-large chunk of coal in the wood-burning stove in the kitchen. Turning the handle on the flue pipe, I turned the damper to the correct position (the adjustable plate inside for controlling the draft) so the coal would burn at a low, consistent temperature. I then tucked the children into bed. Their bedrooms were closer to the kitchen to keep them warmer. I had the back bedroom.

In the middle of the night someone called my name, "Janis!" It jolted me out of a dead sleep. I bolted to an upright sitting position and instinctively responded, "What?" I had no idea who was calling me. I opened my eyes and looked about. The whole room was filled with smoke.

I leaped out of bed and ran through the grey, choking clouds into the front room, my eyes watering. The whole house was full of it. Coughing, my lungs burning, I hurried into the kitchen and saw the problem. The wind had whipped down the stove pipe and blown the damper shut, causing a backdraft. I quickly opened the damper.

Knowing the dangers of carbon monoxide, I raced to the front door and opened it, and then tore through the house opening all the windows. Lastly, I grabbed some towels and began whipping the smoke toward the open front door.

By morning, I had the house cleared, and the children gave no evidence of any toxic symptoms. Had God's voice not called to alert me to the danger, there's no doubt by morning we would have been dead, overcome with the poisonous carbon monoxide fumes.

He is indeed an ever-present help in trouble. Didn't he say, *"Am I not a God near at hand . . . and not a God far off?"* (Jer. 23:24 MSG)

It was especially thrilling that he called me by name. He didn't just try to jar me awake, or call out, "Hey you," or "Wake up!" He used my name—he knew me *that* personally! Jesus said he *"calls his own sheep by name"* (John 10:3).

I rejoice in knowing how much God loves me, and watches over me. He will always be there for me.

> *Fear not . . . I have called you by name, you are mine.*
> *When you pass through the waters, I will be with you;*
> *and through the rivers, they shall not overwhelm you;*
> *when you walk through fire you shall not be burned, and the flame shall not*
> *consume you.*
> *For I am the LORD your God.* (Isa. 43:1-28)

CHAPTER 27

God Didn't Give Up on Me
by
Isaac Fazio
(my grandson)

Never will I leave you; never will I forsake you.

—Heb. 13:5 NIV

My testimony forever will be about God's love and faithfulness. Why? Because he never gave up on me. And my testimony must include my mother who also refused to give up on me, consistently raising prayers to heaven in my behalf.

When I was very young, even though I knew my Bible, I became angry I didn't have a dad. To make things worse, I contacted him by phone and he made it evident he wanted nothing to do with me. I grew so angry that I became destructive at home, at school, and in trouble with the law.

Mentally tormented, I became suicidal and was diagnosed as bipolar. My emotional state, plus the experimental medicine produced a desire to kill everything in my path. In addition, Satan, who *"prowls around like a roaring lion looking for someone to devour,"* found his mark, and hoped to *"steal and kill and destroy"* me (John 10:10 KJV).

Doctors sent me through one facility after another, and at age nine I was admitted to a mental hospital because I was suicidal. I truly wanted to die this time. I felt nobody cared for me, not even my mother. Only later did I realize how much she loved me as she continued to pray, trying to deal with my difficult behavior.

There in the hospital, I decided I would end it all by taking fifty of my prescription pills, the ones that slow down the heart. I knew if I took enough of them my heart would stop. I had hidden them well when entering the facility, and began taking them throughout the day. I remember telling the hospital staff, "Hey, I'm taking these pills—I'm committing suicide!" They didn't believe me.

The last thing I remember is popping the last one—and bam! I fell into blackness. I know where I should have gone, although I didn't understand it completely at the time—to hell, the natural consequence of my life's actions.

I went into a coma, and the doctors gave my mother no hope, telling her I would likely not live. But Jesus met me right when I was falling and I survived, not only because of others' prayers but because God still loved me and had a purpose for my life.

I came out of the coma three days later. My mom explained what happened and then asked, "You know what day this is? It's Easter Sunday."

Wow! What a day for God to resurrect me. But I had a long way to go before I allowed myself to submit totally to God.

I fought against God into my teenage years because I didn't want to give up my old way of life. I used ecstasy, meth, and alcohol, and even dabbled in witch-craft. During that time, God continued to give me messages—even a special dream—where he showed me the dead and withered condition of my soul and presented me with a choice of either continuing to walk down the road of death or to begin the process of restoration.

I paid no attention and decided I would run away from home, live on my own, and demonstrate my self-sufficiency by living off the land for food. I bought camping gear—the whole works, including a tent. I was eighteen and my mother couldn't stop me—nobody could. Yet God made one last attempt to reach out to me.

I flew to Washington and visited my grandmother, who lived four hours from the Canadian border. From her house I planned to sneak across the border, head up to Alaska, and then into Russia.

I shared my plans with her. She tried to talk me out of crossing the border, insisting I would be caught and arrested because of the electronic surveillance.

She showed me maps of northern California, pointing out the number of national parks, trying to convince me I could better live off the land if I headed that direction. I agreed, but only to give her peace of mind. I was not actually intending to change my destination. I decided I could still head for Russia by going up the California coastline to Alaska.

My grandmother loaded me up with addresses of homeless shelters, told me about jobs available at various fishing ports along the way, and gave me some money in case I couldn't trap a squirrel and needed to buy food.

She drove me to Seattle and I took off. My grandmother told my mother later that she cried all the way back home. Neither she nor my mother knew if they would ever see me again. But . . . God had plans.

Before I left home, my mother gave me a pocket Bible. The Lord planned to use that to get to me for I was one of his sheep, and John 10:29 says God protects us from the Destroyer to make sure no one plucks us from the Father's hand.

Two hundred miles later, it was raining and miserable. I was in my tent trying to sleep, but a recurring thought kept me awake: *Read the Bible.* I eventually opened it up and read Proverbs by flashlight. Out of all the Scriptures I could have picked God spoke to me through this one:

> Those who work their land will have abundant food, but those
> who chase fantasies have no sense. (Prov. 12:11 NIV)

I realized I had no sense by running off and trying to live off the land. I was a fool chasing a fantasy. I cried out to God, "What do you want me to do?" In some strange way, I discerned him saying he wanted me to go back home. "No," I told him, "I want to keep going." God answered with silence.

Deep down, I knew I was at the point of no return and had to make the greatest decision of my life. I had no more excuses to run from God. Yes, I now saw myself as foolish, chasing a fantasy of aimless traveling with no end in sight, whether it was Russia or someplace else.

I traveled the 200 miles back to my grandma's house on the money she had given me. She was shocked to see me, but happy. After I shared what happened, she said, "God has opened a door for you now, so you have to return home and do what you must do."

Before I left, I prayed and sought the Lord. I began reading more Bible and study books, and then returned to Texas and voluntarily entered Victory Outreach Christian Recovery Home. That's where my life really began to straighten out with God. He met me there and showed me nothing but love.

The training was admittedly painful and once, early on, I stood on the front porch of the home ready to quit and leave when I heard an emphatic voice say, No! It was the first time I ever heard an audible voice. I knew God didn't violate one's free will, so I recognized it was up to me whether I wanted to obey or not. I stopped myself from leaving and went back inside the building.

Nevertheless, Satan wasn't about to let go of me. While at the home, still battling suicidal thoughts, I headed outside to grab a rope to hang myself. I proceeded to the door and barely put my hand on the handle to turn it when something literally stopped me. Physically, I could not move. The presence of God fell on me so heavy it pushed me down on the floor, and there I sat feeling this tremendous Love. He didn't let me move physically until I made the decision not to get the rope.

Through that Victory Outreach program and the inspired leaders working with me, God pulled all the bad stuff out of my life and freed me of all my addictions and confused thinking. Also, I have no more bipolar symptoms. The Scriptures say those who belong to Christ become a new creation and the old life disappears (2 Cor. 5:17). That's exactly what God did.

> LORD, there is no one like you! For you are great, and your name is full of power[!] (Jer. 10:6)

I am now twenty-two at this writing, assisting a pastor in an inner-city church in Fort Worth, and helping with the youth program and street evangelism. Serving God is my whole life now. All I want to do now is live the rest of my life for Christ and help others also become a new creation in him.

He has called me to be a missionary and has promised me a continent, the continent of Asia, with the purpose of planting churches in every inner city to reach the "lost treasures" hidden in darkness, the drug addicts, gang members and the lost.

God never gave up on me, and neither did my mother. I continually thank the Lord for her. On Mother's Day I told her how much I loved her, and how I now realize that without her consistent love and prayers all those years I wouldn't be alive today. God honored the prayers of my mother, my grandmother, and the many others who interceded for me.

> *Give thanks to the Lord, for he is good; his love endures forever.* (1 Chron. 16:34 NIV)

CHAPTER 28

No One To Turn to But God
by
Tony Estes
(my son-in-law)

Do not call something unclean if God has made it clean.

—Acts 10:15

Hopeless and lost, I sat on the bed in my small apartment in Texas, desperately searching for answers to the overwhelming complexities of life that had brought me to this deplorable point.

The consequences of how I was living years ago had triggered a domino-like reaction, with everything collapsing one upon another until my inner being was lying in complete ruin. It was as though a huge black hole of despair was drawing me into myself, leaving me trapped. I knew there was absolutely nothing I could do to escape the weight of everything crushing in on me. It was a horrible, gut-wrenching feeling, leaving me emotionally heartsick and totally lost.

I could blame no one but myself for my condition. My choices led me to this dark place in my life. As a young man of twenty-eight years, I was incredibly foolish and naïve about life. I didn't understand how wrong choices could have such unimaginable consequences—not only for my life but also for my soul.

There was nowhere to go and no one to turn to, except God. I had always known he existed; I just didn't know how to connect with him.

Clutching the Bible to my chest, I swayed back and forth in sobbing pain, pouring my heart out to God. I pleaded he would somehow intervene and save me from the mess I had become. "Oh God, please forgive me for being such a fool. Show me what I must do. Speak. Let me hear your voice so I know you hear me. I need something from you . . . *anything!*"

I laid the Bible on my lap, then paused. I had an idea. "Lord," I said, "you can reveal yourself to me through your Word. I'm going to open this book. Let my eyes see what you want me to read."

I let the pages fall open, paying no attention to which book it was, as I was pretty illiterate about the Bible. My eyes were immediately drawn to a passage (later, I was able to identify it as Deuteronomy 14) that listed all the unclean animals that were not to be eaten because they would also make the partaker unclean before God. It made no sense to me.

Unaware how Scriptures could be used as metaphors in applying to one's life, I had no idea what eating unclean meat had to do with me. How was that a message from God? Yet, I did not doubt God heard my prayer and was speaking to me. I closed the Bible and reflected on what I had read.

"God," I said, "no offense, but that didn't make much sense to me. Let's try again. Please redirect my eyes to another verse you want me to see, but only from a different part of the Bible."

I opened it again, this time a little past the middle. It fell to the tenth chapter of Acts, and my focus was directed to verses nine through sixteen. I couldn't believe what I saw. To my amazement, this passage also spoke of unclean meats! It told how God lowered a sheet full of unclean animals and told Peter to kill and eat them, with Peter refusing because Jewish law said they were unclean. But God declared in that passage, "Do not call something unclean if God has made it clean."

I sat in awe. Two verses talking about the same thing in two opposite and random places in the Bible. The chance of that happening had to be more than a coincidence. But what does abstaining or not abstaining from unclean meat have to do with my life? And what did God mean about making unclean meat clean?

I looked upward. "God, what are you trying to show me?" No answer came. I concluded I needed to be patient. He would eventually show me what it all meant.

With that I fell asleep.

The next morning, I awakened with a deep yearning in the depth of my being. It strongly compelled me to quit my job and leave for Ada, Oklahoma where my Christian aunt lived. I had to go. I can't explain how I knew to do this; I just did.

I called my parents and told them. They were completely taken by surprise and couldn't understand why I would do such a thing. Despite their objections, I took off.

My aunt lived on a 400-acre farm in a small community. She was happy to see me, and asked, "Would you like to go to church with me on Sunday?" I agreed.

As I listened to the pastor, it was if God had tailored the message just for me. My spirit was completely overwhelmed. When the preacher gave the altar call to receive Jesus, it was like an overpowering force drew me forward. I accepted Jesus into my life and was baptized.

Afterward, I was filled with a profound peace from the turmoil I had been going through. It was like a huge boulder had been lifted off my back. God had answered my prayer, and Jesus was the answer to everything. But just as amazing, I found out afterward why I had felt compelled to go to Oklahoma.

My aunt told me, "During the previous two weeks, when you were going through so much back in Texas as you described, the members of my church told me they had been praying for you the whole time—and I hadn't even asked them to do that."

The whole experience confirmed God heard their prayers. Neither my aunt nor her church had any idea what was going on with me at that time. The Spirit just rested on them to do it, and they determined to keep on night and day until their prayers were answered. Little did they know God was going to bring me to their little church where I would turn my life over to Jesus Christ. I still hadn't figured out the meaning of the scriptures about clean and unclean meat.

I stayed two weeks and tried to get a job, but to no avail. At my aunt's suggestion, I fasted and prayed and asked God what I should do. I was impressed by the Spirit to go to San Antonio. I had no idea why. My aunt was delighted. "My son is there." she said. "He's attending International Bible College. You can connect with him."

Once I arrived and met up with my cousin, God further directed me to enroll at the college. That's when everything became clear. Through my studies, I eventually understood what the two passages about eating unclean meat meant. The bad choices I had made in my life were like eating unclean meat and, as Deuteronomy stated, made me unclean before God. But in the passage in Acts, God wanted me to know that although I had made myself unclean, he could make me clean. He said, *"Do not call something unclean if God has made it clean."*

That day in Ada, Oklahoma's little community church, God made me a new creation when I accepted Christ. He cleansed me and forgave me of all my unclean sins. I also learned from the Bible that from then on, by my walking in his life-giving Spirit, *"there is no condemnation for those who belong to Christ Jesus"* (Rom. 8:1). My crushing burden was lifted!

I am proof that God always hears the prayers of those who put their faith in him. God became accessible to me through Jesus, who said,

> No one comes to the Father except through Me; I am the door
> . . . if any man enter in, he shall be saved. (John 14:6; 10:9)

I walked through that door . . . met Jesus . . . and he made me clean.

> *And with him [Christ] you were raised to new life because you trusted the mighty power of God, who raised Christ from the dead.* (Col. 2:11–12)

CHAPTER 29

A Mormon Missionary for Jesus?
by
Debra Estes
(my daughter)

*Trust in the LORD with all your heart; do not depend on your own understand-
ing. Seek his will in all you do, and he will show you which path to take.*

—Prov. 3:5–6

I grew up in the Mormon Church and loved it. I truly believed it was the only
true church which God had restored to the earth through Joseph Smith. I loved
my heavenly Father and Jesus with all my heart and believed Jesus was at the
head of this church leading and guiding us through his prophet.

Jesus brought my life joy, purpose, and meaning. I wanted to live only for
him and serve him. This desire constantly burned in my heart. So, I grew up
dreaming of being a missionary for Jesus.

I sensed my dream was going to materialize when I was twenty years old
and living in Kalispell, Montana. One day, I was reading my *Campus Life* magazine, which I had subscribed to since a friend introduced it to me during my
high school years. It wasn't a Mormon publication, but throughout the magazine
were ads about opportunities to serve Jesus, such as feeding children in other
countries, building churches, going on youth missions, etc.

One day an ad caught my attention and would not let me go. In big bold
letters it read, "Be part of the team and come build an orphanage for Jesus." It
literally jumped off the page into my heart and spirit. Wow, an opportunity to do
something for Jesus. I had seen similar ads before, but this time, every fiber of
my being said, "I want to do this . . . I *have* to do this!"

Although a Mormon, I felt I would fit in because I loved Jesus, and so did
the people in the ad. I wondered whether I could undertake a mission like this
and not tell people about Joseph Smith and the only true church of Jesus Christ.
But the desire to go do something for Jesus was so strong it made all my questions fade into the background.

I prayed for God s guidance and asked him to stop me if it wasn't his will for my life. Of course, I believed he would approve because it was all for Jesus.

One afternoon I was walking down the sidewalk to a friend's house when a very strong jolt went through my whole body. It forced me to come to an abrupt stop. I literally felt as if I had run into an invisible brick wall. I could not move or take another step. At that moment, these words shot throughout my entire being: *"NO, you are to go on a Mormon mission!"* Wow, it was God and I knew it. He had actually stopped me and redirected my life. I was not supposed to go with the *Campus Life* mission team to build that orphanage for Jesus.

My new destination was now set, and I immediately began preparations. Little did I know what the Lord actually had in mind—he knew this would be the route to bring me out of Mormonism. During the wait for my official call, God continued to confirm that this is what he wanted me to do.

The long-anticipated day finally arrived, and I entered the Missionary Training Center in Salt Lake City, Utah. For the next eighteen months of my life, I believed I was going to be a missionary for Jesus and was filled with great peace knowing it was God's will for me. My dream had finally come true.

I could write an entire book on all the things God used and placed before me during my mission that opened my eyes and heart to the truth of his *real* gospel.

First, I was disturbed by the series of seven lessons we taught to people who wanted to learn more about the church. The first three lessons were about Joseph Smith, the *Book of Mormon*, and the LDS Church. We were told to stop teaching anyone who had not accepted Joseph Smith as a prophet and believed the *Book of Mormon* was true by the end of those three lessons because those two factors were the foundation of the church. The lesson about Jesus and who he truly was did not come until the sixth lesson. I felt strongly that the Jesus lesson should be the first one . . . certainly, not the sixth![1]

My heart began to be heavily grieved and saddened throughout the year because of this, and I soon came to the point where I lost my joy. I had come out here for Jesus, yet all I was doing was teaching people about Joseph Smith and the church. Where was Jesus? I so desperately wanted to hear about and teach about him. In our church meetings on Sundays, I found myself getting up and walking out in tears because I was hearing nothing about Jesus.

Three months before my mission was to end, I knew I could no longer be a Mormon. By that time, I had become a "senior companion" responsible for training new sister missionaries who would accompany me in door-to-door evangelizing. What was I to do? How could I stay in the mission field and train the new recruit assigned to me after everything the Lord had shown me? I was in a dilemma. I prayed about it. Once again, the Lord let me know I was to stay. I didn't know why at the time, but he knew those three months would prove to be a vital part of my journey.

I trained the missionary, and she and I would pray and map out the areas of houses we would visit each day. But something peculiar happened. God began leading us more and more often to the homes of "born-again" Christians.

I will never forget one encounter with a mother whose son had just been saved. We knocked on the door and introduced ourselves, and she invited us in. As the senior companion, I took the lead and let the woman talk first so we could get to know her better. This approach was expected to help us when presenting the church to her.

This woman was so excited that her eyes filled with tears as she shared in detail how Jesus had changed her son's life. He had been addicted to drugs, alcohol, in and out of jail, etc. but because of Jesus had been totally set free.

As she continued to share, I felt God's presence so powerfully that I fought back tears, overcome with the awareness of how Jesus had literally transformed and changed her son's life. When she finished, I thanked her for sharing, proceeded to say good-bye, and left.

My companion and I walked down the road, and I couldn't say anything. I was left speechless, overwhelmed with the realization that it had been Jesus and Jesus alone who had changed that boy's life—not the church—not Joseph Smith—and not the *Book of Mormon*, only JESUS and his saving power.

My companion broke the silence. "Sister Hutchinson, you didn't tell her anything about the church. You didn't say *anything*." It took me a few seconds to reply. All I could say was, "I know." We continued to walk again in silence. I don't know how all of this affected my companion because she had more time to serve after I left. But I believe God was doing a work in her too.

I completed my mission and returned home, marveling at what God had done. My Heavenly Father knew I needed to go on my Mormon mission to realize the error of Mormonism and become free in Jesus.

I started attending a little nondenominational church as I continued my journey out of Mormonism. I say "journey," because it took several years before I was completely free from all aspects of Mormon doctrine and the hold it had on me. But—oh—what an exciting adventure it has been! By trusting in the Lord instead of leaning on my own understanding, I allowed God to direct my path.

And in following that path, I got my joy back!

> *My lips will shout for JOY when I sing praise to you—I whom you have delivered. My tongue will tell of your righteous acts all day long.* (Ps. 71:23–24 NIV)

CHAPTER 30
I'm Forgiven!
by
Debra Estes

*If we confess our sins, he is faithful and just to forgive us our sins
and to cleanse us from all unrighteousness.*

—1 John 1:9 KJV

I had just returned from my Mormon mission, through which God showed me the errors of Mormonism. After requesting my excommunication from the LDS Church, I was attending a small, nondenominational church. I had always been taught, even as a Mormon, that Jesus forgave all our sins. I also knew the Bible taught this and had read the above passage in I John. However, for some reason, I wasn't sure if he had actually forgiven me. Aware of all the sin in my life, it had truly become a heavy load to carry. I was miserable, bound to the point that I had no peace.

I never shared my concern with anyone else, and at times when Christians would be praying for me about other matters, I would simultaneously be crying out within my spirit, *Oh, God, all I want is to know if I am forgiven! Please God, am I forgiven?* I had to know for sure.

A year passed and still no answer. I was in my late twenties when I decided to go to International Bible College in San Antonio to learn more about the Bible and get a handle on Christian doctrine. I desperately wanted to know God's truth—all of it.

One Sunday morning, a group from campus piled in the car like we did every Sunday, and drove to our off-campus church. I nearly didn't go as I was tired from staying up the night before doing homework. But I forced myself to get up, push through, and go.

It was communion Sunday, and as the cup was passed to me, I took it and stared down into the blood-colored liquid. As I did, something unexpected happened.

Everything and everyone around me disappeared—my friends, even the church building. I was there by myself, existing in some kind of spiritual realm. I looked up and above me I saw Jesus nailed to the cross. Looking at the scene, I didn't perceive it as an artist's portrayal. This time it was personal—I knew he was there for *me!*

I continued to focus my gaze on Jesus and the cross, when I saw another person on that same cross with him. Who was it? It was me! I was not only on that cross, but I was somehow inside his body. We had merged and become one.

I continued to watch in awe for some time. Eventually, I saw my body gradually come out from his, come down off the cross, and fuse back into me. Jesus remained on the cross.

No words needed to be spoken to tell me what God wanted me to know. At that very moment, I knew without a doubt Jesus had taken my place and stayed on that cross to die just for me and my sins. I no longer had to stay on the cross. It was then I understood Paul's words: *"I am crucified with Christ, nevertheless I live"* (Gal. 2:20 KJV).

When I looked back down into my communion cup, I found myself once again among the people in the church. Everything returned to normal. I thought of what the Bible said: *"There is no condemnation for those who belong to Christ Jesus"* (Rom. 8:1). I now understood, and my soul thrilled. No more condemnation!

I was never the same after that. I was now free, no longer carrying my heavy load of sin. I knew for sure Jesus paid the price for my sin and I was truly forgiven.

The most remarkable fact of the matter is that he didn't die on the cross just for me. He did it for all those who would call upon his name.

> *He himself is the sacrifice that atones for our sins—and not only our sins but the sins of all the world.* (1 John 2:2)

> *If we confess our sins, he is faithful and just to forgive us our sins and to cleanse us from all unrighteousness.* (I John 1:9 KJV)

CHAPTER 31

My Frozen Shoulder: Should I Testify?

by

Debra Estes

So don't worry about these things . . . your heavenly Father
already knows all your needs.

—Matt. 6:31–32

Doctors don't know what causes someone to develop a "frozen shoulder" (also known as adhesive capsulitis). It just happens. The tissue around the joint stiffens, scar tissue forms, shoulder movement becomes difficult, then slowly and painfully diminishes until the shoulder literally "freezes" and no longer moves at all. Simple chores become impossible. That's what I developed, and it required surgery.

The operation wasn't the hard part since I was sedated for that; much more difficult were the months of painful physical therapy and exercise to get my shoulder and arm back to normal functioning. During all this, the medical expenses grew.

I worried about the bill but agreed with Luke 10:7 that *"the laborer is worthy of his hire."* I appreciated having a doctor who knew exactly what to do and believed he deserved to be paid in full no matter how difficult it would be for me.

At that time in my life, I was a divorced single mother raising two children. I worked for the school district in the kitchen cafeteria preparing, cooking, and serving breakfast and lunch to students. I purposely took the job even though it didn't pay much so I could have the same days off as my children. I couldn't afford daycare. I was paid once a month, about $659, obviously living by the grace of God from paycheck to paycheck. He also provided a way for us to be on the Section 8 housing program, for which I felt very blessed. I was meticulous with my finances and kept excellent records of everything. I knew exactly where every penny went and always paid my bills. Then came the bills for the doctor, the surgery, and physical therapy.

My insurance from work covered part of the bills, but I still owed thousands of dollars. I sat down and carefully calculated how much I could pay each month and realized it would take me nine years to pay off those bills. But I knew I could do it and determined to pay them in full.

At my final appointment with the doctor, my shoulder had healed and was moving well, and I looked forward to his releasing me so I could return to work. I was just about to step down from the exam table when I noticed the doctor was about to say something.

"Debra," he asked calmly, "how are you going to pay for all of this?"

I was surprised he even asked that question as I knew the clinic's accounting department handled the financial end of things. Very businesslike and in a very confident voice, I proceeded to share my plan for payment.

"I can pay ten dollars a month for sure," I said, "and there is no need to worry as I will never miss a payment. It might take me a while but I will do this until it is paid off."

I will never forget what the doctor said next.

"Don't worry about it," he said. "You don't owe me anything."

I sat there completely overwhelmed. As far as I knew, the doctor knew nothing of my life or finances. I had never said anything about it to him, and we had never discussed anything even closely related to it. Unsure if I heard correctly, I asked the doctor to confirm what he just said. Sure enough, he repeated it.

I tried not to cry but failed. With my eyes full of tears, I jumped off the exam table. Without a second thought, I gave him a huge hug and thanked him. He evidently didn't expect my response. He looked stunned for a minute but then gave me a smile that lit up his whole face. No words were necessary. His whole being relayed the words, "No," he said, "thank YOU for letting me do this for you."

Driving home, I praised and thanked God while still wondering if the doctor would really follow through with his promise. I decided to wait a few days and then call the billing department to casually ask what my balance was. Sure enough, I owed nothing. I was so excited about what God had done for me—and also so grateful to the doctor—that I wanted to tell the whole world. I especially wanted to share this testimony at church the following Sunday.

I eagerly arrived at church, anxious to tell everyone what happened. The time for testimonies came, but seconds before I was to get up and share, I began looking around at my church family. It was a small church, and we were all close.

I knew many of my friends were struggling, barely making it financially, some worse off than me.

Doubts flooded into my mind: *Why hasn't God done the same for them? I want to tell them to trust God and he will do it for them too. But what if he doesn't? How can I explain that?* All my testimony would do is leave them feeling sad and depressed, wondering why God hasn't come through for them. *How can I share this gift with them when so many are hurting?*

I remained seated and did not share my testimony until several years later when I remembered Jesus told a man in Luke 8:39 to *"Return home and tell how much God has done for you."* How could I hold back when God wants us to testify to his goodness? Now, I no longer hesitate.

I have learned that God works in unique ways with each person. The blessing he gives me may not be identical to what he gives someone else; nevertheless, he is true to his Word and always comes through for his children. And hearing how God has blessed others when I still have needs does not discourage me; rather, it encourages me. Sharing your testimony can do the same for others. My experience lets me know that all things are possible with God. Isaiah said:

> Thank the Lord! Praise his name! Tell the world about his wondrous love and how mighty he is. (Isa. 12:4 TLB)

Therefore, I continue to tell others about the mighty things God has done for me. What a freedom it has been to share.

No, I don't always know who will be encouraged by my story, but I can't let that stop me. My story might encourage one person and cause their faith to explode and bring to pass the miracles and mighty works God has in store for them.

He never fails to satisfy us each morning with his unfailing love. We should, as Psalm 90:14 says, *"sing for joy to the end of our lives."*

> *But my life is worth nothing to me unless I use it for finishing the work assigned me by the Lord Jesus—the work of telling others the Good News about the wonderful grace of God. (Acts 20:24)*

CHAPTER 32

"I Need a Guitar!"
by
Debra Estes

Take delight in the LORD, and he will give you your heart's desires.

—Ps. 37:4

One of the joys and passion of my life is playing the guitar and singing for Jesus. For years, I used the classical guitar I had obtained when it had only one crack in it. But eventually the wood cracked in several places and the neck broke in two preventing the strings from being tuned. It was beyond repair.

Strangely, I didn't pray about the situation or ask God to provide another guitar. I just accepted that my playing days were over. Perhaps someday, in the far-off future, I might be able to get another one. How, I didn't know, as I was living from paycheck to paycheck with two children to support. But God knows the secret desires of our heart, and he knew mine.

One day, I was driving home from work when I saw a garage sale sign, an unusual sight on a weekday. Typically, if you see one during the week, it's because someone forget to take it down after the weekend. I love garage sales but wasn't interested in checking out this one. Even if the sale was still going, it was the end of the day, so the good stuff would be gone by now.

But suddenly, with no forethought or reason, I found myself turning and heading down the road to check it out. It felt like someone else was literally doing the driving. Why was I doing this? I was tired, wanted to go home after a long day at work, and had no desire to go to a garage sale.

But I continued following the signs down strange roads where I had never been before, as if a magnet were drawing me to a planned destination. After driving for five minutes, I saw the house. Sure enough, there was a garage sale going on. I got out and began looking, not really knowing why I was there.

As I had expected, not much stuff was left. But right in the middle of the sale was the most beautiful classical guitar I had ever seen! The guitar lay inside a hard case, cushioned by a soft black lining, and the sun shone on the satin wooden finish which didn't have a scratch on it. I knew guitars well enough to know it was very expensive. It looked so new, I had to ask if it was even for sale. The man's response stunned me.

"I bought it brand new," he said. "I intended to learn to play it but never touched it. I just want to get rid of it. I can let you have both the guitar and case for only fifty bucks."

At that moment, I *knew* in my spirit this was from God. Wow, what a deal! The guitar was there just for ME! It was the exact kind of classical guitar I wanted . . . the color, the shape . . . everything! And to think I hadn't even asked God for a guitar. I counted this a miracle!

All the way home I praised and thanked him for leading me to this guitar, literally driving me there when I had no intention of going. I couldn't help but think of two scriptures:

> "A man's mind plans his way, but the Lord directs his steps and makes them sure." (Prov. 16:9)

> "Your Father knows exactly what you need even before you ask him." (Matt. 6:8)

CHAPTER 33
The Filing Miracle
by
Debra Estes

Then you will call, and the Lord will answer; you will cry for help,
and he will say: here am I.

—Isa. 58:9 NIV

I work for a mental health clinic as a medical-records specialist. My job is to locate and pull clients' medical charts for the doctors, file daily paperwork, and process record requests from other facilities, hospitals, attorneys, and the clients themselves.

In the room where I work, there are over 7,300 client files dating back to the year 2000. Imagine a huge library but instead of books, the shelves are loaded with thousands of file folders. There were shelves upon shelves of files. Eight shelves crammed with files cover two of the walls from floor to ceiling. Filling the middle of the room are six free-standing rows, five-shelves high, filled with files on both sides. Archived files fill the shelves on the back wall, approximately 100 boxes, with twenty-five to thirty files in each box.

Forty of those boxes of archives were recently brought to the clinic from the previous owner's off-site storage unit. During the ownership transition, the lists detailing the contents of each box was lost, so we didn't know which box contained which client's files. My next big project was to manually go through each box, index the names, and computerize a master list.

One morning I received a call from a client who desperately needed copies of her records for an important legal matter. Hearing the urgency in the client's voice, I knew this needed to be done right away, so I reassured her I would call her back as soon as I located them.

I pulled up the client list on the computer and looked up the caller's name to get her six-digit file number. I proceeded to go to that section, but the file was not there. I didn't panic at this point, as things sometimes get misfiled. I looked through all the files with the same last two numbers. Not there. I thumbed through each file on all the rows within ten numbers of the file I was seeking. Not there. I checked to see if someone had reversed the last two numbers. Again, no.

I doublechecked the file number on the computer. Yes, I had it correct. I checked the "discharged" file section. Nothing. Again, I searched the indexed list of client names from the sixty archive boxes. Not on the list. I retraced my steps several times, looking where I had already looked, hoping I had just missed it the first time. No such luck.

I noticed the message light blinking on my phone and found two urgent messages from the client. I reached for the phone and slowly dialed her number.

"I'm so sorry," I said, "for not getting back to you sooner. It's taking me a little longer than I thought. There are still more files I need to look through." I couldn't tell her we had lost them.

She repeated to me how important the records were to her and told me how two other clinics where she had been a patient had been unable to find her records. Beginning to cry, she asked, "Why can't you find them? I feel like everyone is trying to prevent me from getting them."

"Please don't be upset," I reassured her as calmly as I could manage. "Your records are here, and I will find them."

I spent the rest of the morning and into the afternoon searching for the client's file; I even began looking on random shelves, hoping and praying I would stumble across it. Still no file.

I finally stopped for a late lunch at a small table between two aisles of shelves near the back wall. As I sat down, I closed my eyes and cried out to God in desperation.

"I've done everything I know to do," I said, "but can't find her records anywhere. Can you please help me locate them?" I emphasized how important it was, concluding with, "God, I know you know exactly where her file is. If you could please share that with me, I would so much appreciate it."

I opened my eyes, and they landed on an archive box on the bottom shelf a few feet from where I was sitting. It stood out among all the rest because the lid of the box was missing. There were about twenty folders in that box with each client's name written in black magic marker across the folder tabs. One folder was raised slightly above the others, and from this distance, the name of the tab looked like . . . could it be?

I leaped out of my chair and made a beeline to the box. If my heart could have turned a cartwheel, it would have at that moment. Up close, I read the name on the tab. It was the file I had been searching for all morning. That client's name wasn't on the list of the sixty archived files—her file wasn't supposed to be in that box, yet there it was! I pulled it out, and with tears in my eyes began praising and thanking God.

This was truly a miracle! What were the chances of my chair being turned exactly at the right angle for God to position my eyes to fall upon "that" file in "that" box, which "just happened" to be missing a lid? I was overwhelmed at how amazing God is. He even raised the folder slightly so I wouldn't miss it.

Every time I recall what happened, it brings tears to my eyes and a special knowledge that, "Yes, God is real, and we can trust him for anything." He cares about every problem or difficulty we face, no matter how big or small. All we have to do is call out to him and ask, then simply open our eyes and he will show us the answer!

You may ask me for anything in my name, and I will do it. (John 14:14 NIV)

CHAPTER 34

Entering into the Joy of the Lord: A Revelation Miracle
by
Debra Estes

Don't be dejected and sad, for the joy of the LORD is your strength!
—Neh. 8:10

I knew the Scripture *"the joy of the Lord is your strength"* had to be true because I'm a Christian and I believe in God's Word. But a problem existed . . . I didn't have the joy this Scripture promised.

I had been married and divorced and was now raising two children by myself. Life was hard. With the challenges, difficulties, depression, and dissatisfaction with my life, I knew that I would have never made it without God. Nevertheless, the joy the Scriptures spoke of was missing in my life. I needed it. But I had no clue how to find it.

I was twenty-seven years old and attending a Christian singles group. One month the group invited a guest speaker who focused on Nehemiah 8:10, *"the joy of the Lord is your strength."* I listened to him quote the Scripture and became angry. Deep within my inner being I heard myself scream, *You're lying—the joy of the Lord is not my strength! How can those words be true? I'm a Christian, and I don't have it.*

By the time the meeting was over, anger utterly consumed me. Unable to contain myself any longer, I turned to my friend and blurted, "Yeah, right—the joy of the Lord is my strength. So, where is it?" My friend, startled, said nothing. Yet, even as I said it, I knew God's Word was true. And at the moment of that inner acknowledgement, a supernatural confirmation of the truth of God's Word shot through my entire being with power. But I still didn't have this so-called "joy."

Confused, my anger slowly gave way to determination. I would not rest until I had found this "joy" of the Lord." Nothing would stop me.

A few years passed but with no joy. In hindsight, I know I hadn't found the joy because I had no concrete plan for how to discover it. But how could I formulate a plan without knowing what steps to take?

I came to the point where I desperately needed to know if there was any purpose to life—a reason for me to exist if there was no joy. If I could find that purpose, it might be the key that would unlock the promised joy. What was the point of continuing if there wasn't any? Oh, I knew all the cliché answers about life having purpose, even several Scriptures, but they were all empty words. Researching the subject only brought a variety of guesses and opinions of others. I continued to make it a matter of prayer.

One day, I was reading Philippians 3, and verse 8 startled me. Paul said everything he had accomplished in his life was worthless when compared with the infinite value of knowing Christ Jesus his Lord. What a profound conclusion and perception!

I kept reading. Every word leaped off the page. They literally exploded the truth of Paul's discovery deep into my heart. Yes, it was the only answer to what made life purposeful and what would bring joy: TO KNOW HIM!

The revelation of this wove itself into every fiber of my being. It was why I had been created and who God intended me to be—a worshiper who truly knew him in an intimate way. The light dawned. There it was . . . the purpose for my existence. Something shifted in my spirit, and I knew the course of my life was about to be changed forever.

My plan began to materialize. It would consist of how to know Jesus and how to enter his presence because Jesus said, *"ENTER thou into the joy of thy lord"* (Matt. 25:21 KJV). Even David understood this: *"In thy presence is fulness of joy"* (Ps. 16:11). Therefore, the only way joy in life could be experienced was to "enter" his presence . . . and truly knowing *him* could only be acquired by entering in a way I had never done before.

I knew what steps needed to be taken. Excited, I mapped out my plan in detail. In a notebook, I listed the procedural steps for *how* to know him.

My plan was to rise one hour earlier every morning to spend time with God, and to also dedicate an hour in the evening after the children were in bed. The first fifteen minutes I played my guitar and sang praise songs. Sometimes I would just listen to praise music.

The second fifteen minutes I read the Bible with new eyes, not just reading the Scriptures about God, but searching specifically to *know* him—*what* he is . . . *who* he is. For example, God doesn't just *do* acts of kindness, he *is* Kindness.

God doesn't just *do* acts of love; he *is* Love. God doesn't just *do* acts of holiness; he *is* Holy.

Knowing his attributes would allow me to more fully experience HIM. And if I didn't understand something in his word, instead of trying to figure it out with my brain I waited for the Holy Spirit to reveal it to me—and the Spirit amazingly came through.

The next segment of time was spent in thanking him, praising him, sometimes just sitting in silence and focusing on an awareness of his holy presence. Sometimes I felt nothing but kept going, determined. I followed this plan for several months, evolving into a year. I never gave up . . . even when I wondered if I was getting anywhere.

One day I was sitting at my kitchen table meditating on God and reflecting on the day. I felt happy and at peace. *"Wow!"* I thought, *"This is different. I am really happy."* Nothing around me had changed. Same life, same situations, same troubles and challenges each day. What made the difference?

It was being in his presence every day, knowing who he is and understanding his attributes. I experienced the BIGNESS of God—his holiness, majesty, all-encompassing power, and ability to make all seeming impossibilities possible.

Yes, my problems continued to be big, but God was BIGGER. I knew without a doubt that it was no effort for God to take care of me and all my challenges. I could absolutely rest in that.

Totally overcome with the presence of God in that moment, I felt an incredible, indescribable JOY. Tears began to flow. I now understood 1 Peter 1:7–8, for I had *"joy unspeakable and full of glory."* Real joy! God's Word echoed a confirmation in my spirit: "Yes, in my presence is fullness of joy." My prayer from so many years ago was answered. It was a revelation miracle. The "joy of the Lord" was now my strength!

Years have passed since then. He is still the purpose of my existence, and every day I experience his joy as my strength. Thank you, Lord, for showing me the path which leads to the fullness of that joy.

> *Thou wilt shew me the path of life: in thy presence is fulness of joy; at thy right hand there are pleasures forevermore.* (Ps. 16:11 KJV)

Introduction to Appendices

Delivering Effective Testimonies

Let them praise the Lord for his great love and for the wonderful things
he has done for them.
Let them exalt him publicly before the congregation.

— Ps. 107:30–32

The Joshua Project showed you how to effectively present, preserve, and perpetuate faith stories within your family and for future descendants. I hope you are excited to begin your project, recalling the many divine encounters you have kept private for so long.

But, as you create your Joshua Project, remember that your testimonies should not be limited to just your family. Everyone loves to hear stories about God, especially a first-hand account. The stories affirm his reality and love, and the effectiveness of personal testimonies can especially be seen in church meetings.

Testifying in church is not to be undervalued because "faith comes by hearing" (Rom. 10:17). New converts may be in the congregation, and hearing your testimony will bolster their faith and confirm they made the right decision in coming to the Lord. Your testimony may also touch lethargic Christians who need their heart and spirit revived, or motivate mature believers to begin sharing the many years of God's activity in their lives. Unbelievers may also be sitting in the congregation, and your testimony may reach them maybe more effectively than direct evangelizing methods. Personal testimonies are designed to deliver a powerful impact. This is what God wants.

There is one primary difference between sharing with our family and giving public testimony at church. When we share with family we can expand on the details, taking all the time we wish. However, this won't work at church.

There are time restraints in public gatherings, and you must know how to draw forth the most important points of your testimony and not ramble on with unnecessary details. Do not let this limitation discourage or keep you from sharing your stories publicly. But do spend some time learning how to deliver effective testimonies. The step-by-step instructions in the following sections will help you prepare.

Appendix I will describe how you spiritually benefit from testifying, and also details of what others are hoping to hear from your stories. It shows the change that can result in a church community because of your declared witness, and clarifies the difference between impromptu (spur-of-the-minute) testimonies versus scheduled ones.

Appendix II presents a step-by-step outline to equip you to deliver the perfect timed testimony (usually three minutes). It includes dos, don'ts, and precautions. Thus prepared, you will be ready for any occasion when you are asked to testify, and be assured you can confidently follow through on David's admonition to *"exalt him before the congregation"* (Ps. 107:30-32).

Appendix I

Problems and Benefits of Church Testimonies

Someone once said, "It takes a brave church to allow testimonies." Why brave? Because there are several concerns in public presentations.

Pastors worry that individuals might ramble on for twenty minutes (see Appendix II). But they also worry that someone might relate a vision that is way out in left field, embellish their account, criticize how the church is being run, or focus on themselves instead of glorifying God.

One pastor admits:

> Testimony is a risky practice . . . it takes a confident church to introduce testimony, I suspect—one willing to face the unpredictable and to release some control. But it is in the very release of control that the blessings come.[1]

The release of the blessings is the focus. However, you may assume that your testimony will produce the same kind of blessing to all the individuals in the congregation. Not necessarily. They will indeed be blessed; but the effects will differ with each individual.

Various Types of Blessings

Testimonies can lead to a wide variety of blessings because a congregation consists of a wide variety of mindsets. All may be Christians, but not all have the same methodology in their thought processes. Oftentimes, we forget this.

Therefore, the Holy Spirit invokes diverse responses and reactions relevant to each person's predisposition and where they are in their life's journey. Here are examples of blessings that can occur for these various groups:

- **New converts.** Hearing a testimony thrills their souls. Through it, the Holy Spirit can confirm they made the right decision in accepting Jesus as Lord and Savior. In the future, they anticipate God giving them a similar experience to the testimony being declared.

- **Listless Christians.** Testimonies may jolt this group out of their lethargic condition. A personal testimony can touch their hearts and stimulate a desire to revive their spiritual life. They may devote themselves to a more active prayer life and desire to acquire a closer intimate relationship with Christ and the Holy Spirit they once had.

- **Academic Christians.** Some who have previously conceived of God as an impersonal abstract spirit may, through hearing a testimony, begin to perceive him for the first time as an authentic and personal spiritual reality involved in close intimate activity with believers. The Holy Spirit can shift their thinking from an academic and intellectual bent to a spirit-touching experience, instilling a longing for a closer presence of God in their life similar to what the testifier is describing.

- **Matured believers.** Hearing someone's witness can spark a recall of what God has done for them throughout the years, and energize a new resolve to begin sharing more of their own testimonies.

You, as testifier, will not always know who has been touched by your testimony, or in what way, but that is irrelevant. Your task is to witness and glorify God. It is the Holy Spirit's job to touch whom he will and produce the needed effect in them.

Benefits to Testifiers

Although sharing one's testimony encourages and imparts faith to others as *The Joshua Project* makes clear, "hearers" are not the only ones who receive a blessing. Testifiers also benefit.

They are blessed even before they present their testimony to the congregation; for example, when they prepare ahead of time for a scheduled presentation (impromptu testimonies are discussed later). During their preparation time, they contemplate more deeply the godly event they plan to talk about, which often triggers memories of everything God has done for them in years past. This invokes a gratitude and love that often brings them to their knees.

They may also sense the Holy Spirit validating their decision to testify and glorify God to others rather than keeping their experiences as concealed memories for their own savoring. Further, when testifiers speak to the congregation, the sound of their own voice, declaring what God has done, gives them a strong, resonant inner witness to that event, reinforcing God's powerful reality, love, and faithfulness.

Benefits for the Church

When testimonies are regularly shared, a dynamic can occur within the church that melds the whole body of the church community in a holistic way. This effect is not planned. It just happens.

When individuals open up their innermost lives and share testimonies of how God entered into their everyday life to help with problems other members can identify with, it binds everyone together in a camaraderie that is more deeply relational than the usual detached exchanges of "Good morning, how are you?" or "God bless you, brother."

Pastor L. Daniel of New Haven, Connecticut, wrote the following in *The Christian Century* after instigating testimony time in his church:

"Newcomers often commented on what they learned from the testimonies. This feature added an element of anticipation to worship and helped us to grow deeper in our relationships with one another. For each of us who have participated, the reflection and clarification has been a transforming experience in itself. For the worship service, it creates an atmosphere of openness and trust, and a sense of personal connection. A member named David commented: "I think the practice of testimony has been an important part of the revitalization of our congregation."[2]

The Subject of the Testimony

The greatest testimony is, of course, a person's salvation experience. However, God doesn't stop there, and neither should we. Why? Because our lives are full of periodic stress dealing with the harsh realities of existence. In them, we turn to God for help when dealing with sicknesses, financial problems, tragedies, and other distressing concerns. Everyone is eager to hear these testimonies of what God did to help, because they are common problems they also deal with. Testimonies give them hope.

Impromptu or Scheduled?

Occasions for impromptu invitations to testify often occur when a pastor discovers unexpected time to fill. While good, this avenue can cause problems for members.

The first problem is that the request is usually accompanied with the statement, "Keep it brief," without the pastor explaining how long *brief* means.

With no definition, most members become flustered, and feel pressured to come up with something fast. If members do think of a testimony, they perform lightning-speed mental gymnastics to see how to whittle it down to only three or four sentences. What can they really communicate when being that brief? How can they fully explain without giving all the details they feel are so necessary? What parts should they include? Exclude? What if they should exceed the time period of "brief" and exasperate the pastor?

On the other hand, members also worry if they *don't* testify, they'll be letting the congregation down and won't be giving God his due. They may also be concerned that if they don't say something, others will think God isn't doing *anything* in their life!

These problems can be remedied in two ways:

- If they suspect impromptu testimonies are a possibility, individuals can prepare a short testimony ahead of time, using the "Instructions for a Three-minute Testimony" found in Appendix II.

- The church could schedule a once-a-month meeting dedicated solely to testimonies, and state the time allowance—which will often be longer than three minutes. Members will flock to these.

The prescheduled setup will prove more productive than impromptu testimonies because it offers the following advantages:

- Volunteers can sign up ahead of time (or be assigned by the pastor) so they can give more thought and prayer about which account they should share, and have time for the Holy Spirit to direct them.

- A specific time allotment for delivery of testimonies will normally be stated, for example ten minutes or less per testifier, depending on how many are scheduled.

- Members will have plenty of time for preparation.

- The church can also provide guidelines and clarify what should be included or excluded.

- Members have time to ponder and discern what the take-away value of their testimony should be and focus on that. This reduces the chances the congregation will be fascinated only with the dramatic element rather than the spiritual message.

- Members will have ample time to reread their presentation to make sure it glorifies God, not themselves; also, make certain they are not choosing a faith story solely for its sensationalism.

While impromptu testimonies have their place, scheduled testimony meetings are highly recommended. Members will have time to prepare ahead, and can give a well thought out testimony directed by the Holy Spirit.

The Calendar Time Ban

Another quandary often makes members reluctant to share. It is the sometimes spoken-but-often-unspoken time ban on testimonies. This ban is not referring to "clock" time but "calendar" time.

At churches and conferences, it is not unusual to hear a speaker say when inviting testimonies from the floor, "Now, don't tell something that happened to you five or ten years ago; tell what God did for you last week." Even if not stated publicly, this sentiment has come to be generally understood in many churches and conferences, forcing many to repress outstanding testimonies they would like to share. They wonder, "Why should godly accounts from earlier years be disqualified?"

This calendar ban, however, has good intentions. Its objective is to show that God is currently operating in people's lives. Nevertheless, the restriction negatively relays two concepts:

- Testimonies about God from earlier times are not worth hearing or speaking about.

- Something must be wrong with you if God hasn't currently performed some out-of-the-ordinary, testimony-worthy event in your life in the last few weeks. This presents an uncomfortable moment for those whose life may be going pretty smoothly and can't think of anything exceptional God did currently (or even needed to do).

This time ban especially affects mature believers who have accumulated many testimonies over the years. They feel they must ignore earlier events, leaving them no opportunity to share outstanding and effective, faith-promoting testimonies. They definitely have one or more of those kinds to share, but they may have occurred six months, a year, or even many years ago. Yet, sharing those testimonies would violate the understood calendar limitation.

Acts of God toward his children are worthy of a testimony regardless of when they occurred. *Nothing* God does should be discounted. Therefore, when inviting testimonies from the congregation, this calendar ban should be lifted, making it clear that all faith-building testimonies from any time period will be allowed. By doing so, more members will be blessed with an increase of faith, and it permits the testifier to be faithful to God's mandate to witness of his mighty works.

God's Other Reason for Testimonies

Previous chapters in *The Joshua Project* explain several reasons for why we should testify, but there's another perspective from God's point of view to consider.

God said his acts and words, both in the Bible and to us individually, are designed to accomplish one thing—they are not to "return to him void"—meaning they are meant to influence others.

> So shall my word be that goeth forth out of my mouth: it (also my acts) shall not return unto me void, but it shall accomplish that which I please, and it shall prosper in the thing whereto I sent it. (Isa. 55:11 KJV)

How can the words or acts we have received from God prosper in influencing others if we keep silent about them? Our testimonies of what we have received are meant to reinforce, strengthen, and prosper the faith of others and glorify the Giver. When no one testifies to what he has done, whatever the recipient received will return to God void, and not accomplish the intended purpose; that of affecting more people than just the one who initially received it.

God continues to give more testimony-qualifying experiences to us because he:

- longs to make himself known. (Josh. 4:24; Ezek. 39:7; 2 Kings 19:19 and others);

- desires for us to *"praise [him] for the glorious grace he has poured out on us who belong to his dear Son."* (Eph. 1:6); and

- wants others' faith in him strengthened from hearing our testimonies.

God's overarching purpose in giving a divine encounter can be seen in the vision of the risen Christ given to Saul on the road to Damascus. Jesus' appearance was not solely to give him a spectacular vision. It was so Saul would have something to testify about afterward (Acts 9).

Similarly, we receive blessings from God, not only because of his love, but so we have something to testify about.

Taking all the above into account, the conclusion is that it takes a brave church to allow testimonies because of many concerns. But by working them out, individual members and the church are benefited, and God is glorified.

APPENDIX II

How to Give Your Testimony in Three Minutes

*Always be prepared to give an answer to everyone who asks you to
give the reason for the hope that you have.*
—1 Pet. 3:15

Testimonies of changed lives are one of the greatest witnessing tools we have. A testimony's objective is to influence others and glorify God. Whether declared in a church meeting or one-on-one witnessing, they serve to honor God, confirm his reality, impart one's faith, and illustrate what it means to be a Christian. This is the focus for all testimonies.

What does it mean to "glorify God?" For converts, it means declaring God's loving grace and salvation by telling their story of how God rescued and saved them. It is their eyewitness (I-witness) account of how their lives changed as a result, giving God the credit.

For long-time Christians, it may be a personal witness of an answered prayer, a medical cure, or some other miraculous event from God and how it enhanced their faith. Therefore, the following instructions will equip you to give the perfectly timed testimony.

The guidelines are gleaned from my own insights and from various church websites. Dos and don'ts will be provided, along with tips on how to divide three essentials into one minute each to conform to the three-minute standard often stated by churches. What are these three essentials?

For the convert, they are (1) your life before Christ, (2) how you came to Christ, and (3) your life after Christ, with less than thirty seconds for an opening (brief introduction of yourself) and closing. For the long-time Christian, relating a miracle, answered prayer, or other supernatural event that solved a problem. Both are detailed further below.

Two Platforms for Presenting a Testimony

There are two ways you may be asked to share a testimony:

- **From the floor.** This usually means impromptu testimonies are given by members in the congregation who volunteer, stand by their chair, and testify when handed a mic.

- **A pre-planned testimony meeting.** In this situation, the pastor may ask for volunteers, or may assign certain members ahead of time. If this is the case, three to five minutes is acceptable, although the pastor may state a longer or shorter time based on how many are slated to speak. Be sure to ask.

Two Kinds of Testimonies

Not everyone's testimony will contain the same content. But in general, there will be two types of testifiers.

- **The long-time (or mature) Christian.** The long-time Christian will typically not be talking about their conversion experience, which will have occurred many years prior. Rather, they may tell about a miracle, answered prayer, or other supernatural event, attesting to how God is an ever-ready source of help in time of need.

- **The convert.** New Christians will usually share their conversion experience, how happy they are for their decision, and how accepting Christ has changed their life. Under no terms should a church pressure a new convert to testify if they are not ready.[1]

Should You Memorize?

Some suggest memorizing a three-minute version. My view is that after you write it down, you shouldn't necessarily memorize word for word; otherwise, your presentation will sound stilted. You should, however, memorize just enough here and there so you can give what you have prepared without rambling or straying off course while adhering to the time limit. Using notes for key points is fine.

Converts may be helped in their preparation by at least memorizing the three main headings of a testimony outline: "BEFORE" (your life before Christ), "HOW" *(how you came to Christ)*, and "AFTER" *(your life after accepting Christ)*. They can create short subheadings within those.

Long-time Christians who may be testifying of an answered prayer or other godly event can do the same. But, the *"before, how,* and *after"* will differ according to the special event they are testifying about. "Before" may be describing the prior problem; the "how" is what they did to ask God, and the "after," describes how God came through.

Specific Instructions for Three-minute Testimonies

Coming up with a short testimony on the spur of the minute can prove trying for many. How can you come up with something quickly, provide necessary backstory, and whittle it down without leaving out something important? The answer is, you probably can't unless you do what 1 Peter 3:15 admonishes: *"always be prepared."*

The following guidelines will help you determine the essential details to include, what to leave out, prevent you from rambling, and keep you within the allotted time. (The *before, how,* and *after* will fill the three-minute standard; the "opening" and "closing" should add thirty seconds or less to the three minutes.)

Below each of the three headings are suggested ideas of what you can include. Take the time to read Paul's testimony to King Agrippa (Acts 26). He used the same model of *before, how, and after.*[2]

The examples below are primarily formulated for the convert's testimony. But application to long-time Christians is also referenced by using LTC (long-time Christian) italicized in brackets, even though they will be testifying of something other than conversion. However, many of the suggestions for the convert will also apply to the LTC; so, in that case no LTC comments are necessary. The word "event" will refer to the occasion when God came through for you.

OPENING. **Convert: Brief introduction of yourself.** *[also, LTC]* (30 seconds or less)

BEFORE. **Your life before Christ.** *[LTC: What was happening before your godly event occurred?]* (1 minute)

Suggestions

- Tell what your life was like before you experienced Christ *[LTC: the problem you were experiencing before the event.]*

- What was your attitude, emotion, situation? *[LTC: same].*

- Did something major happen to put you in crisis?

- Were you searching for something before accepting Christ?

- Were you experiencing wrong relationships (sought through gangs, drugs, money, etc.), life's meaning, security, peace, friends, purpose? *[LTC: Was something missing from your life? How did you try to fill it before resorting to prayer?]*

HOW. **How you came to Christ.** *[LTC: Tell how you prayed, how God came through, and how it changed your faith.]* (1 minute)

Suggestions for the "How":

- What made you decide on Christ? Someone's witness? Introduction to a church program?

- When did you sense Christ? *[LTC: when did you realize God was doing something?]*

- What was your main difficulty in making the choice for Christ? *[LTC: Did you have any difficulties prior to the godly event?]*

- What were the mental or physical steps you took? *[LTC: Did you think prayer was the answer at first?]*

- Where were you when you made your decision? *[LTC: Where were you when God came through?]*

- Did you have a special experience in prayer about Christ? (It's okay if you didn't.) *[LTC: Did you have a supernatural experience in prayer during or before the event? Or, did God direct natural circumstances to solve the problem?]*

- Was it through a friend's witnessing? How did you first react? *[LTC: did you believe God would answer your prayer before he acted?]*

- How did you feel when you turned your life over to Christ? *[LTC: how did you feel after God came through?]*

AFTER. **Your life after Christ.** (1 minute)

Suggestions

- How is your life different? *[LTC: your life after the event]*

- Has accepting Christ made a difference in your life, actions and attitudes? *[LTC: Has the event changed your life in any way?]*

- Do you feel closer to God?

- How does his forgiveness make you feel? *[LTC: How do you feel since?]*

- What did you gain from the experience? *[LTC: What did you gain from the event?]*

- Do you still struggle with previous problems? Be honest. Don't put on a false front and claim life is perfect since accepting Christ. *[LTC: Do you still struggle with faith even though God came through on this event?]*

*"If we are still trying to make church, faith, and Christian living real" says Becca Vandekemp-McLellan, "testimonies need to get real, too. We can't act like our struggles magically disappeared when we accepted Christ. Anything but the truth does a disservice to ourselves, to truth, and to each other . . . Struggle is a reality. Temptation is a reality. Failure is a reality. Yes, even for those who are actively walking with Christ . . . real faith lives aren't just rainbows and sunshine. Let's stop acting as if they are."[3]

CLOSING. Purpose of the closing. (30 seconds or less)

- The closing should focus on Christ in a simple way so others will want to know him more personally.

- Make sure everyone knows that Jesus is the answer to any problem of sin. *[LTC: Jesus is the answer when problems arise.]*

- Summarize your testimony and what you learned.

- Attest to how God answers prayer and is an ever-ready source of help in time of need.

- Glorify God. You can use applicable Scriptures, or your own words.

- Challenge members to allow more of God into their lives (or unbelievers to accept Christ.) *[LTC: Challenge the congregation based on what you have shared.]*

The tips above should equip you to be fully prepared whenever an occasion should arise.

A Few Things to Remember

- Refer to everything in the first person (I, me).
- Don't generalize. Give examples to put flesh on your story.
- Focus on what was previously happening to you without feeling the necessity of going into details that are overly sensational; nevertheless, include feelings and personal insights.
- "Be honest," states author, Mary Fairchild. "The simple truth of what God has done in your life is all the Holy Spirit needs to convince others of God's love."[4]
- Can include humor; it increases attention.
- Smile and show you are happy.

A Few Precautions

- Be sure to pray before your preparation, so you can deliver it in the power of the Holy Spirit.
- Do not lie, exaggerate, or bend the truth.
- Examine your motives. Make sure it is to glorify God.
- Don't glorify a sinful past (prison, drugs, murder, etc.) in an effort to present something dramatic, believing it will go over better. While some mention of it may be necessary, it's more important to include how accepting Christ has changed your life. Paul's admonition should be remembered: *As for me, may I never boast about anything except the cross of our Lord Jesus Christ* (Gal. 6:14).
- For the LTC, focus on how God answered your prayer or how God supplied your need.
- Avoid statements negative to the church and staff.

- Don't tear down another denomination you may have come out of, even if its beliefs are unbiblical; rather, refer to the institution with a more general type statement.

- Do not turn your testimony into a preaching opportunity.

- Do not use words non-Christians won't understand without defining them, even when testifying in your own church. There may be visitors present.

- Don't load your testimony with too many Scripture verses. Two at the most.

- Don't be long-winded—stick to the assigned time.

- Try to avoid *uhs* and *ahs*, sniffing, or other nervous habits.

- Don't make it sound like you lived the perfect life after your conversion and all your weak points, temptations, and failures disappeared in a puff of smoke. Admit if you "slipped" after conversion and how Christ is helping you deal with it.

Writing out your testimony based on the outline, partially memorizing it, and having it prepared ahead of time in an organized fashion (you can have notes for key points) will prevent verbal stumbling, getting rattled, extraneous matter, and overly long testimonies.

By following the above guidelines, you will be ready for any occasion when asked to testify, and can be assured of a confident delivery whether it's "impromptu" or for a "prescheduled" meeting.

> *Our testimonies of God's interventions in our life should not fade into obscurity from lack of declaration.*

Notes

INTRODUCTION

[1]J. Warner Wallace, "Updated: Are Young People Really Leaving Christianity," Cold-Case Christianity, January 12, 2019, www.coldcasechristianity.com/2018/are-young-people-really-leaving-christianity/; quoting from Josh McDowell and David H. Bellis, *The Last Christian Generation* (Green Key Books, 2006). LifeWay Research says that two-thirds of the 70 percent of all youth in mainline religions who said church will not play a part in their adult lives return to "some level of church involvement in their late 20s or early 30s." Nevertheless, the one-third remain lost to the culture.

[2]Wallace, "Updated: Young People." See also, Aaron Earls, "Most Teenagers Drop Out of Church as Young Adults," LifeWay Research, January 15, 2019, www.lifewayresearch.com/2019/01/15/most-teenagers-drop-out-of-church-as-young-adults.

[3]"Parents and Pastors: Partners in Gen Z Discipleship," Research Releases in Millennials & Generations, Barna Group, July 17, 2018, www.barna.com/research/parents-and-pastors-partners -in-gen-z-discipleship/. (my italics).

[4]"Teen Role Models: Who They Are, Why They Matter," Research Releases in Millennials & Generations, Barna Group, January 30, 2011, www.barna.com/research/teen-role-models-who-they-are-why-they-matter/.

[5]Josh Mulvihill, *Biblical Grandparenting: Exploring God's Design for Disciple-making and Passing Faith to Future Generations* (Bloomington, MN: Bethany House, 2018), 38.

[6]Mulvihill, *Biblical Grandparenting*, 24, 146.

[7]Bob Smietana, "Young Bible Readers More Likely to be Faithful Adults, Study Finds," LifeWay Research, October 17, 2017, www.lifewayresearch.com/2017/10/17/young-bible-readers-more-likely-to-be-faithful-adults-study-finds/.

CHAPTER 1

[1]Genealogies were crucial for people in Joshua's day. Only people who could prove their Israelite lineage could claim family land. It was especially

important for Levite priests, who needed to establish their descent from Moses' brother, Aaron, the high priest. If they could not, they were banned from officiating in the Temple and receiving the applicable benefits. To serve without proof of lineage would be a sacrilege. The "begats" were especially necessary after the Babylonian exile, when the Jews returned to Jerusalem to rebuild the Temple. Some Levites could not prove their lineage, and the consequences were great. (see Neh. 7:61–64).

CHAPTER 2

[1]Alex Harris and Brett Harris, *Do Hard Things: A Teenage Rebellion Against Low Expectations* (Colorado Springs: Multnomah, 2008), Kindle.

[2]I did not include the response from my son who lives far away from me because he has been unable to visit me. My other adult son is with the Lord.

[3]"Grandma's Song," by Kimberly Clark, YouTube music video, 4:28, January 25, 2016, www.youtube.com/watch?v=RSmaZ6UqfAc.

CHAPTER 3

[1]The six mandated feasts listed here exclude Hanukkah and Purim, which were introduced later by the Jewish people. They understood the value of remembering and knew exactly how to ensure it. Purim was created as a memorial to remind them "from generation to generation" about gaining relief from their enemies due to Queen Esther's efforts. They did not want "the memory of what happened [to] die out among their descendants" (Esth. 9:28). Hanukkah was created to remember the eight-day rededication of the second temple in Jerusalem.

[2]Michael Youssef, *The Hidden Enemy: Aggressive Secularism, Radical Islam, and the Fight for Our Future* (Carol Stream, Ill.: Tyndale, 2018), 53, Kindle.

[3]J. Warner Wallace, "Updated: Are Young People Really Leaving Christianity," Cold-Case Christianity, January 12, 2019, www.coldcasechristianity.com/2018/are-young-people-really-leaving-christianity; quoting from "Choosing a New Church or House of Worship," research findings from Pew Research Center 2015.

[4]Wallace, "Updated," quoting Mk. M. Gray, "Young People Are Leaving the Faith. Here's Why," *Our Sunday Visitor Newsweekly*, 2016. Research by CARA National Study (Center for Applied Research in the Apostolate) www.coldcasechristianity.com/2018/are-young-people-really-leaving-christianity. From a study of Catholic Church youth 15–25 who left their church. The figures parallel studies of defecting youth from other Christian denominations.

[5]Wallace, "Updated," quoting from Josh McDowell, David H. Bellis, *The Last Christian Generation* (Green Key Books, 2006).

CHAPTER 4

[1]James Bishop, "74% Of Doctors Believe in Miracles, 55% Have Seen Them," Reasons for Jesus (website), May 6, 2017, www.reasonsforjesus.com/74-of-doctors-believe-in-miracles-55-have-seen-them. An American survey of 1100 physicians, researched by HCD Research and the Louis Finkelstein Institute for Religious and Social Studies of The Jewish Theological Seminary in New York City.

[2]Gretchen Anderson, "Miracles, Divine Healings, and Angels: Beliefs Among U.S. Adults 45+ with Hispanic Oversample," 2008. Survey conducted for *AARP The Magazine* and *AARP Segunda Juventud*, www.assets.aarp.org/rgcenter/general/miracles_08.pdf.

[3]"Most Americans Believe in Supernatural Healing," Research Releases in Faith & Christianity, Barna Group, September 29, 2016, www.barna.com/research/americans-believe-supernatural-healing.

[4]C. S. Lewis, *Miracles: A Preliminary Study* (New York: Harper Collins, 2009), 88.

[5]James Watkins, "God Is Never Late—But He Sure Is Slow," Hope & Humor / James Watkins (website), accessed March 9, 2019, www.jameswatkins.com/articles-2/hopeful/neverlate/.

CHAPTER 5

[1]*The Confessions of St. Augustine*, by St. Augustine, trans. Edward Bouverie Pusey. Kindle edition, 2012; a Public Domain book,116. "This book was converted from its physical edition to the digital format by a community of volunteers." ASIN: B00AQM75SC.

[2]A. B. Simpson, *Days of Heaven on Earth*, entry under "September 29" (Project Gutenberg, March 27, 2009) eBook 28416, p. 276, www.gutenberg.org/files/28416/28416-pdf.pdf accessed October 20, 2019 from www.gutenberg.org/ebooks/28416 and www.gutenberg.org/files/28416/28416-pdf..

CHAPTER 6

[1]Kendra Cherry, "Long-Term Memory—Types, Duration and Capacity," verywell mind (website), October 6, 2018, www.verywell.com/what-is-long-term-memory-2795347. (Italics mine.)

[2]Cherry, "Long-Term Memory." (Italics mine.)

[3]Kendra Cherry, "The Misinformation Effect and False Memories," verywell mind (website), March 13, 2019, www.verywellmind.com/what-is-the-misinformation-effect-2795353.

CHAPTER 15

[1]"Jesus Loves Me" by William B. Bradbury, 1862; public domain.

[2]Spencer W. Kimball, *The Miracle of Forgiveness* (Salt Lake City: Bookcraft, 1969), 324–325. Quoted by Eric Johnson, "A Closer Look at Spencer W. Kimball's *The Miracle of Forgiveness*," Mormonism Research Ministry, accessed April 9, 2019, www.mrm.org/the-miracle-of-forgiveness.

[3]"The Love of God" by F. M. Lehman; public domain. Verse 3 was written by Jewish poet, Meir Ben Isaac Nehorai, in A.D. 1050. See, Ben Glanzer, "Music of the Message: The Story of 'The Love of God,'" Ministry (website), accessed July 24, 2019, www.ministrymagazine.org/archive/1950/09/the-story-of-the-love-of-god.

CHAPTER 20

[1]Billy Graham, *Angels: God's Secret Agents* (Word Publishing, 1986), 36.

[2]Graham, *Angels*, 27.

CHAPTER 24

[1]Graham, *Angels*, 27.

[2]Dr. Jane Glenchur, *Seven Secrets to Power Praying: How to Access God's Wisdom And Miracles Every Day* (Bloomington, Minn: Chosen Books, 2014), Kindle.

[3]Graham, *Angels,* 36, 26.

CHAPTER 25

[1]"Great is Thy Faithfulness" words by Thomas O. Chisholm, music by William Runyun (Hope Publishing, 1923). Under public domain as of 2019.

CHAPTER 29

[1]To gain more converts, the LDS Church has since rearranged their lessons to put Jesus first.

APPENDIX I

[1]L. Daniel, "Sharing Faith Stories in Worship," The Christian Century, April 4, 2006, 20–25, http://www.religion-online.org/showarticle.asp?title=3391. Permission requested May 16, 2017.

[2]Daniel, "Sharing Faith Stories."

APPENDIX II

[1]For the problems resulting from pressuring an ex-Mormon to testify, see Chapter 10 of Janis Hutchinson's *Out of the Cults and into the Church* (Grand Rapids, MI: Kregel, 1994), 198–99.

[2]Opening: verses 2–3; before: verses 4–11; how: verses 12–20; after: verses 21–23; closing: verses 24–29. (Acts 26)

[3]Becca Vandekemp, "What We Get Wrong When We Give Our Testimony," Relevant Magazine, updated October 22, 2019, http://www.relevantmagazine.com/god/what-we-get-wrong-about-giving-our-testimony.

[4]Mary Fairchild, "How to Write Your Christian Testimony," Learn Religions (website), July 2, 2018, https://www.learnreligions.com/how-to-write-your-christian-testimony-701445.

THE END

About the Author

Janis Hutchinson is an award-winning author of both fiction and nonfiction. Awarded "Writer of the Year" (2008) by the American Christian Writers Association, her books, articles, and short stories have appeared in national and international Christian magazines, on blogs, and in newsletters of various church ministries in Russia, Mexico, and Spain.

Graduating *summa cum laude* and as *distinguished student* with an MA in theology, she has taught Bible classes at both the church and college level. She is a frequent guest speaker at Christian conferences and on Christian TV and radio programs, served twelve years as a mentor for a Christian counter-cult ministry (Institute of Religious Research), and continues worldwide mentoring via email.

A Mormon for thirty-five years, Janis was saved by grace after God enabled her escape from a Mormon offshoot group that held her prisoner for nine months because she refused to renounce the Christian Jesus (her story of how God enabled her escape is on her blog).

But foremost, Janis is a mother and grandmother. Her adult children and grandchildren are Christians, but her concern over the maintenance of their faith, coupled with a need to share her decades of experiences of receiving God's extraordinary blessings and healing miracles, brought her to discover an overlooked biblical method that proved productive in enhancing and strengthening their faith. Thus, *The Joshua Project* was born.

Widowed twice, Janis has raised three children, all of whom have come to personal faith in Christ. She is retired but teaches a Bible class and speaks locally. She now resides in western Washington but misses her native southern California beaches with their white sands, smell of salt air, squawking seagulls, and the inviting energy of ocean breakers.

If you enjoyed this book or found it useful, I'd be grateful if you'd post a short review on Amazon. Your support really does make a difference, and I read all the reviews personally so I can get your feedback and make my writing even better.

Thanks again for your support!

OTHER BOOKS BY THE AUTHOR

Available at Amazon and other internet book sites

Out of the Cults and Into the Church: Understanding and Encouraging Ex-cultists (Kregel Resources, 1994)

The Mormon Missionaries: An Inside Look at their Real Message and Methods (Kregel Resources, 1995); Second edition (Cross and Pen Ministries, 2012)

Misioneros Mormones: Lo nunca dicho de sus verdaderos metodos y mensaje (Editorial Portavoz, 2000)

Unfinished Justice, historical suspense novel inspired by a true story (Cross and Pen Ministries, 2015)

Website: www.JanisHutchinsonBooks.com

Facebook: www.facebook.com/janis.hutchinson1

Blog: wwwJanisHutchinson.blogspot.com *(no dot after the www)*

Twitter: twitter.com/JANISHUTCHINSO1

Linkedin: www.linkedin.com/in/janis-hutchinson-a7670845/

Email: JanisHutchinson@comcast.net